The Best American Short Plays

2002–2003

The Best American Short Plays

2002-2003

edited with an introduction by
Glenn Young

APPLAUSE THEATRE & CINEMA BOOKS
An Imprint of Hal Leonard Corporation
New York

The Best American Short Plays 2002–2003
Edited with an intoduction by Glenn Young

Published in 2010 by Applause Theatre & Cinema Books
An Imprint of Hal Leonard Corporation
7777 West Bluemound Road
Milwaukee, WI 53213

Trade Book Division Editorial Offices
19 West 21st Street, New York, NY 10010

Printed in the United States of America
Book interior by UB Communications

ISBN: 978-1-55783-719-6 (cloth)
ISBN: 978-1-55783-720-2 (paper)
ISSN: 0067-6284

www.applausepub.com

For
Giannina Braschi
and
Tess O'Dwyer,
two dramatic forms
not short on anything

contents

introduction
by Glenn Young

Theater stepped out of the mist of ritual sacrifice millennia ago, but the principle of sacrifice can never itself be replaced. Twenty-five hundred years after Creon's call for Antigone's sacrifice, our stages are still enthralled by its spirit. Ritual and sacrifice once were one and the same, but even as the artist replaced the deed with the act, the human need to witness and contemplate it remains—even if only in living metaphor on a stage. The Christian tradition is founded on such a premise: Christ suffered that in sacred contemplation of his sacrifice his followers may live.

When Willy Loman's wife cries out, "Attention must be paid," she's not talking about attendance at the local theater. She's not bidding up a subscription at the silent auction. It's not as observers that she calls us to account, but rather as fellow communicants in life's dark mysteries. She demands we join in the sacred circle of direct, unmediated experience—the very thing that ritual sacrifice used to supply our human psyche.

The plays that follow are short—short on time, short on words, short on breath—but not short on the magnitude of human experi-ence. A tragedy is a tragedy whether it occurs in one act or five acts.

These brief plays are direct conduits for our modern selves to tap into and renew our ancient ritualistic needs. The dramas are unquestionably brief, but emotionally full, and derive their potency from a timeless well of human experience. The ancient Greeks didn't have our iPods, but we share the same emotional wiring, the same primal limbic platforms that connect us to the visceral requirements of drama.

This collection is bookended by two such powerful dramas, geographically and temporally half a world apart, and yet plugged into the same psychic territory as Aeschylus and Miller. In both, young people are threatened by the established authority figures of their communities, and they must become outlaws, iconoclasts, simply to save their own skins. In *The Beauty Inside*, Yalova, a fourteen-year-old girl is first raped by a neighbor and then drowned—out of shame—by her own brothers, left for dead in a drainage canal. And when she has the audacity to cry out to be saved by passing strangers, her enraged mother can think only to berate and kick her for the "shame" she has brought on the family. In Le Wilhelm's *5:15 Greyhound*, a middle-aged mother shepherds her teenage daughter and son to a bus stop, stealing out in the middle of the night, so that one of them might escape the brutality of their father. In the first instance, the young woman is herself the sacrifice—to preserve the family honor. In the second, it is the mother who accepts that she will be savagely beaten when she returns home. It is the sacrifice that rivets us to the stage. How can people be so cruel? Our outrage fuels our meditation. How can people find the courage—as the young girl does to keep her baby; as the teenagers do to board that bus. This is the ritual for us in the audience, to share these powerful timeless emotions with the participants in the pageant.

In neither of these plays does the paternal tyrant show his face. Yet his absence makes his threat all the more terrifying and omnipotent. No one man could represent the tyranny as potently as this collective looming specter. The paternal despot has the full weight and power of society behind him. His power is not only absolute, but unimpeachable. Both of these plays take place in recent time, but the enemy they face is older than the Greeks. It is feudalism in its unadulterated form, come down to us through the ages, asserting its absolutism simply by dint of tradition and force. It takes great courage not only to stand up to it, but even to imagine it can be challenged. Paternalism is City Hall squared. It is tough to beat. And yet, a young, pregnant fourteen-year-old girl and a couple of young American teens somehow find the will and the inner strength to oppose what they know is malevolent and unjust, despite their lifelong indoctrination to the contrary.

These two plays live on the shores of Jung's stream of consciousness. There's no longitude or latitude that can explain the human heart when it erupts in venom. One of these teens is a Muslim living somewhere in the Middle East; the others are two Christian American kids living in the fifties. And yet they are blood relatives, all three of them. It is not religion that they are rebelling against—it is history itself, the primal instincts of brutal men, which knows no national bounds, respects no religious tenets. But instead manipulates and torments the tenants until they fall into paternalistic line. The playwrights in both plays bestow upon their characters a dignity that finally transcends the undertow of tradition.

The reader is invited to a festival of insight, provided by all the plays chosen for this volume, whose source is timeless, but whose language is today.

The Beauty Inside
by Catherine Filloux

This community's illusion of sanctity spreads a thin veneer of "honor" over the dark, horrific grain beneath. The citizens of this Turkish town will commit any atrocity, up to and including murder and infanticide, to maintain the sacred illusion of equilibrium. This is a one-act play because subsequent acts are unimaginable.

What mother would incite her raped daughter to suicide? Did the Greeks invent a more viperous maternal being than Catherine Filloux gives us here? And yet...as her contemporary myth spreads out its dark tapestries, we cannot help but recognize Yalova's mother—though a subject of the stain, a conduit of it—as still not the source of the stain. Ms. Filloux's powerful poetic talisman functions here like a bookmark to hold the ancient place, and our place, in the primal and ongoing tale of man's inhumanity to woman.

Society is the all-potent protagonist here to whom all the players must sacrifice. The playwright captures a scene in which the characters attempt to blot out the action before it begins. The societal dharma requires that such a story as this one be obliterated and sanitized before it can be heard and folded into the larger communal narrative. The societal chant drums beneath the action: silence, silence. And the mechanism of the action is as brutal as the silencer on a revolver. Nothing is heard, nothing seen, nothing stirred. The play takes up a tragic tempo toward ritual obliteration, as grave in this world as Antigone was in hers.

We hear two strains of narrative: Yalova's exceptional cry picked up by her deus ex machina attorney, Latife. The play's action, like its Greek antecedents, is itself in conflict, simultaneously to expunge and to expose. The seductive glistening shimmer of the river belies the turbulent savagery of its polluted waters.

While Filloux gives us a hopeful ending, the audience remains uneasy about the future. Yalova's savior is real enough, but temporary—she must leave her client's hospital room eventually. Latife's existence has the feel of wishful illusion—a convenient super heroine to save the day. We cannot realistically project a place or time where the girl will be safe from the savage undertow of her upbringing. But let us give the girl's fate the benefit of the doubt. What happens to her sisters? Her child inside?

Brown
by Cherie Vogelstein

"One toke over the line, sweet Jesus," wafts to mind in a Vogelstein debauchery. She is Empress of the Dramatic Sting. So, mind her invitations. When she's on her very best manners, start backing away. She welcomes us with all the civility she pays to all the marks in her trade. She extends the most banal of propositions: a cup of coffee, a scrap of small talk. Her propulsions start ever so meek and mild out of well-washed dramatic denim. But out of that blue—KABLOOEY! The Holocaust—BOOM! Bestiality! Incest! She stacks her deck with just enough standard face cards to make this deck of jokers appear straight. The corporate job interview segues ever so archly first into sophomoric romp, then to savage farce, and ineluctably to its grim denouement.

This feline Fellini plows the same Central Park fields as the rest of us, but where most pick up used condoms and the odd well-chewed tennis ball, Ms. Vee turns up skulls in trenches of perverse desire.

The job interview might be the inspiration for all other dramatic absurdism. It is after all the site of the first Kafka franchise. Or perhaps Ms. Vee snatched a gnarled gambit out of the Marquis de Sade's handbook: twisted tightrope walk, with one's life literally hanging in the balance. Ms. Vogelstein gleefully takes this machinery to its horrible, inevitable conclusion. Dismemberment, brutal humiliation, psychological torture, deceit—welcome to the corporate world, Peter! Can you give as good as you take? Can you brown-nose us without us even knowing it? Corporatedom's most respected skill. Sure, quite a job is done on the poor lad, his nose thoroughly rubbed in the Brown of his alma mater, but he does pass through the gauntlet, does after all get the job. Yes, a happy ending. His mother must be so proud.

and everybody else
by Scott Organ

Yuppie Dave tries picking up yuppie Jane with his line about the poor puppy dying in the street at the last party he attended. He leaves out the part about his doing squiddly to save the mutt. Anymore than he does anything to save his wife from getting plastered inside, where he left her to chat up Jane. Turns out the dog was saved by somebody else.

As long as neither listens much to the other, just connecting the odd dot to his/her own solipsistic monologue, they are in perfect unison about everything. Each is looking for a quickie opp—the feature film of their romance is shot by cell-phone camera. The street where they meet is the land of instant intimacy, where emotions ejaculate prematurely to the vibe of the party music inside. Their conversation echoes down the block, toward next weekend, and the next neck to impress with their cold lips.

Time was, people socialized at parties to meet others. Now, in the chat-room age, we socialize to find ever more flattering reflections of ourselves. The suburban backyard is the child's traditional playground, but since the pale-skinned kids are now indoors all day, the adults have wandered out the back jalousie door. A child will fill a backyard with imagination—a castle, a spaceship. These adults fill the backyard with their own banal emptiness. Dave and Jane are soul mates, or, rather, soul-less mates. It's not socializing they need, but purpose. Both found what they both needed: nobody.

Queenie
by Murray Schisgal

"Wagged heedlessly on the strings of a mad puppeteer," Lawrence Albertson, at sixty-two, finally feels his libidinal leash slacken. His Pavlovian years of subjugation to the call of testosterone steadily relents. At last, he is free to commit to a healthy, mature, long term, relationship, unfettered by "the distended abomination sulking between [his] legs." And he does commit himself unstintingly and without condition. To his dog, Queenie. Yes, he's not the self-centered caveman of yesteryear; he's a modern fellow who can forge a primary monogamous relationship where divorce is unthinkable. Laurence Albertson, megawatt entertainment attorney, takes succor and counsel from that doggy he bought in the window. Of course, the fact that the source of his only security and affection in female form is utterly dependent on him, speaks not a word, and obediently follows his every order, leads one to think that perhaps this gent's preparations for renewing ties with mature American womanhood may be a product of his restricted diet.

The sum total of his transformation is this: Larry has metamorphosed from a sex-driven egotistical lifestyle to a sexless egotistical lifestyle. He's gone from picking up models from his casting couch to finding a domesticated miniature canine model in a store window. Lawyer Albertson is an exemplary model of a "successful neurosis." If you can make your fantasy life work, it's a form of benign madness. Is Schisgal asking us to believe good old Larry? One wonders if even Queenie believes him. She, unlike we, is a captive audience. If Queenie were to magically metamorphose into a real woman, like Galatea, one suspects that poor Larry would run for his life.

Told from many other perspectives, Larry is living one miserable, lonely, meaningless life. In another play, Larry would have his solitary birthday bash, then go home and bash in his brains. But Larry is such a good advocate, such a good manager, he manages to sell himself to himself. He's the true self-made man.

Most one-person shows creak and sag and squirt artifice from every orifice, burning off credibility as they contort themselves unconvincingly into a one-person ecosystem. Not Schisgal's play. Laurence Albertson has excellent cause for his private discourse with his dog, Queenie. First, no one else is worthy of his company; his supreme egotism trumps all other relationships. No one else would put up with a man whose life is a running soliloquy. And that's part of Schisgal's schtick of genius. Albertson's life has been one long one-person play. In most solo plays, we asphyxiate with the lack of other voices. Not here. One cannot conceive another voice contaminating Albertson's all-consuming space.

Another way to look at it, this is actually a two-character play, but one actor isn't getting scale.

Reunions
by Billy Aronson

At their high school reunion, the alumni mostly returned with a canned impromptu screed about how great things turned out for them. Aronson responds to the eternal question: "Is there life after high school?" with the throwback: "Yeah, but we turned into characters from our grade school primers." The graduates in this warm, thoughtful comedy don't grow up so much as they transmogrify into fairy tale characters. They don't so much get promoted into life as take a leap backward into fantasyland. Nancy's a giraffe; Rich is a pirate, but no match for the super pirate Paul. Connie is the first female Santa Claus.

There's obviously something retarded about their development. Once they run out of their set speeches, there's nothing left to say. The loop just rewinds and starts over again. They adopt these fairy tale narratives to cover up the void underneath.

The class loser, Alan, ironically, stands out as the most real in the class. Alan alone knows he's gone nowhere. He has endured, sustained a real loss, but still has the instinct to celebrate what's real, while his classmates celebrate behind their respective fantasies. Alan is the only character who doesn't armor himself with a full psychic costume so we may catch a glimpse of the humiliation the rest of the guests are desperate to avoid. When he starts dancing with Nancy, the giraffe, her head in the clouds, one wonders if, as the music ends, she might not luckily bend her cheek toward his.

Captain Abalone
by Adam Kraar

In Adam Kraar's kaleidoscopic prism, along the beach two bodies pick up the glimmers of two lifetimes, playfully sharing and reflecting each other's light as if sunset were not just over the horizon. A nurse pushes her patient, Abe, to the beach to visit ancient sandcastles of their youths. In their intimate compression comes acrobatic release. Out of Abe's wheelchair cartwheels an Adonis. Out of the nurse's blurred cataracts, the gods have granted her hindsight of her long-lost lover here, in the global womb, on Paradise Beach.

Promises never kept and memories bottled up, they uncork their inner vitality with a vigor nobody in the audience will mistake for an athletic metaphor. When on this landscape of eternal rebirth, Abe declares, "I'm fourteen in my pants and my chest...I'm invincible. See!," there is a visceral timbre to his voice. No hearing aids required. They are rejuvenated re-visiting the protean scene where we all began, crawling out of the sea.

Kraar has put a seashell up to our collective ear, and from its core, we hear the surf in Bali, in Ceylon, in Rio, in Paradise. We tend to agree there is "no other beach, no other world" than this. We glimpse our own erstwhile selves and the shells we are destined to become.

Are the events on this beach wishful thinking or magic realism? Have Abe and the nurse truly burst through the bonds of aging, the chains of time, to frolic freely in refurbished bodies? There is something rejuvenating about a beach. It is, after all, where we all began, crawling out of the sea. The shore has long been a border between the real world and the mysterious world. All things seem possible with sand between your toes, the sun shining in your face.

The Changing of the Guard
by Amy Staats

Mama Sue has imagined a grand tour mimicking the annual pilgrimage she made with her late husband. In this fantasy itinerary, her two granddaughters aren't women with their own interests but young ladies whose manners will naturally reflect the decorum of their good fortune.

Mama Sue lavishes on the young ladies the keys to London: the best hotel, the finest cuisine, every comfort anticipated.

These are two very different generations, however, dreaming of entirely different realms. Eleanor is the princess of her own anarchic realm—as spoiled as any real princess, taking umbrage at her grandmother's audacious command she arise before her hangover subsides. Nor will she deign to countenance those dead relics her grandmother marches them to: "Buckingham Palace is boring. It's a boring, ugly castle. It's just a building with stuffy old people saying old stuffy things." She prefers instead the threadbare talismans of happening Abbey Road and Whitechapel's postmodern exhibits. To her grandmother, Eleanor values hovels over jewels. And, like any good suburban princess who likes to slum, Eleanor doesn't reject the triple-brocade sheets or the silver service in her five-star hotel.

In the first half of the play, the sisters are on one side of their hotel room door while Mama Sue scolds them from the corridor. That door and the barrier it represents needs to open in order for these two generations of powerful women to acknowledge each other. When the door finally is breached, it is as if they see one another for the first time. As they nibble on their scones, an unorthodox communion unfolds.

What starts as a standoff ends in a detente with open hearts. What starts as an adolescent rebellion against their grandmother's power trip becomes an acknowledgment of their own rigidity and selfishness. And they see too that the palace may be more than a corny tourist stop, may be a place that celebrates courage and defiance. Perhaps most persuasive is Mama Sue's argument: "Don't you realize those old stuffy people were young once too? They had lives ten times richer than you could possibly imagine. Why do young people insist they were the first? You have no idea. No idea at all." Bite by bite, the girls come to understand that their trip to London was not so much a tourist trap but an embrace of continuity and their own fate.

Hermaphrodite
by Annie G.

As Jeffrey plans his excavation and preservation of an ancient temple honoring Hermaphrodite, he contemplates various aspects of himself and his origins. The big dig here is an internal one. His invitation to his macho corporate-raider mama comes at a time when she is herself conflicted and bewildered about her own place in life. The stated rationale for their meeting is to discuss the funding of Jeffrey's archeological mission, but simultaneously they examine her own rather schizophrenic history through the various layers and impulses of his mother's gender and cultural programming. Her own battle to create a super hermaphroditic American CEO has come at the cost of her identity.

She is among the first generation of women who strove to "have it all." That is, live both a successful, traditional woman's life as well as a man's. To be the perfect mom and the successful business titan. And—she's done it. Now comes the bill. Jeffrey, her son, by all outward appearances is himself an admirable success, a talented archeologist. And yet, he does seem just a bit cold, just a bit opportunistic. He does treat his mother more like a potential sponsor than a relative. Perhaps Chris has indeed transformed herself into a Greek god—powerful, but distant and pitiless, with her offspring fearing more than loving her. So, should she have stuck to her pots and baby bottles? Not at all. Only that there are inevitable trade-offs in life, no matter what course you follow, no matter how spectacularly you succeed.

Jeffrey's intellectual base camp is anchored to the premise that we can never "know enough about ourselves." His mother, Chris, looks at herself in the mirror and discovers she has "no reflection." She has expunged so much of herself to get ahead that she herself had disappeared. Chris is perpetually running on empty. "I need a refill," she calls out. She's made zillions but feels broke. She has nipped and tucked away so much of herself in plastic surgery that the face that's left is unrecognizable. She hears the dreadful echo of meaninglessness inside her hollowed shell.

Annie G.'s accomplishment is that Chris is both perpetrator and patient. She is both the nut and the bolt that fastens this monstrous mutant together. Her psychic dismemberment here reminds us that the superficial changes in our make up are not merely skin-deep. There is a reason Hermaphrodite was a god.

When his mother's relentless drive ultimately burns out, she agrees to fund the dig, but the living artifact she may save is herself.

Sada
by Bruce Levy

Some might observe that *Sada* goes on a touch too long for a short play. Some might point out that *Sada* is a touch too sentimental, or perhaps a trifle too melodramatic to represent drama of the twenty-first century. It's true that good old-fashioned storytelling often goes out of style. *Sada* is a good example of why that's a shame.

Genuine heroes are scarce in modern drama. Like God before them, they seem to have died. But here we encounter a true hero. When everything in her society is disintegrating, as her family and even her own body betray her, Sada remains a genuinely, unflinchingly good person. She immediately spots that Angel, the young thug who breaks in to rob her skimpy apartment, is "a good boy."

Where years of social workers have dismally failed this young man, kindhearted, aging Sada succeeds in the span of one act. Administering to the confused thug with tea and cake, Sada not only saves herself from him, but—for a brief while at least—he from himself. And then, just when she's performed the miracle, bringing Angel back into society, society barges in and spoils everything. First, the fuzz bust in, then, to make matters worse, Ira, the long-lost son who never calls his mamma, picks this night to pick up the phone. For a while, Sada is a match for all of them, holding them all at bay like a wounded bear defending her cub, but even her great strength can last only so long, and she loses the fight. But what a noble effort.

5:15 Greyhound
by Le Wilhelm

While the family patriarch sleeps, two maternal figures assert their quiet redemptive force. Mrs. White negotiates her daughter's escape from her husband's crushing domination. Sister, Mary Alice, and brother, Tom, stand in the cold, with their mother hovering solicitously, awaiting the Greyhound bus that will carry at least one of them away from the domestic violence at the hands of dad at home. The mother is like a desperate mother bird, knowing she can save only one of her chicks from the circling falcon. After leaving her children at the bus stop in the predawn hours, as she makes her way home in the dark, Mary Alice shows her own maternal spark, as she had planned all along to give her brother the first break to freedom. But he rebels at going, and subjecting his mother and sister to the horrible fate he knows is waiting at home when Pop awakes. This is an escape to freedom that could only take place under cover of night, during the precious hours when Mr. White's X-ray eyes are mercifully closed. The sacrifices Mrs. White made to engineer her children's release from bondage will be made painfully clear as the sun rises to expose her plot and her husband's wrath.

So much love, so much sacrifice in the presence of such brutal unthinking, unyielding patriarchal power. Sitting in the audience, you want them to buy a gun, not a bus ticket. But this is the fifties. Pop still holds all the cards legally, socially, religiously, you name it. It's still a man's world.

The play's drama is made as much from what it is not as what it is. The defiance is so gentle, so filled with dignity, that if one didn't listen carefully, one might mistake it as a leave-taking after a family holiday visit. The act of defiance is not marked by outrage or obscenity; it is not vindictive or vengeful. There are no angry oaths of retribution taken against the father. No soliloquies about the injustice of their lives. It is, instead, in this delicate etiquette that Le Wilhelm etches his own brand of dramatic transition from one life to another. Like the torch that signals the coming of Agamemnon, their farmhouse lantern hails a new world approaching on the 5:15 Greyhound.

The Beauty Inside

Catherine Filloux

Catherine Filloux

Catherine Filloux is an award-winning playwright who has been writing about human rights and social justice for the past twenty years. Her plays have been produced in New York and around the world. Filloux wrote the book and lyrics for *Where Elephants Weep* (composer: Him Sophy), a musical, which received its world premiere in Phnom Penh, Cambodia. She is the librettist for *The Floating Box: A Story in Chinatown* (composer: Jason Kao Hwang), selected as a Critic's Choice in *Opera News*. Awards include: PeaceWriting Award (Omni Center for Peace), Roger L. Stevens Award (Kennedy Center), Eric Kocher Playwrights Award (O'Neill Theater Center), Callaway Award (New Dramatists). Filloux's plays are published by Playscripts, Inc., and her recent anthology, *Silence of God and Other Plays*, is published by Seagull Books as part of the In Performance series. Filloux is a co-founder of Theatre Without Borders and has served as a speaker for playwriting and human rights organizations around the world. Visit http://www.catherine filloux.com.

cast of characters (3 women)

YALOVA, 14-year-old daughter of Peri

PERI, Yalova's mother, clever

LATIFE (pronounced La-tee-fay), lawyer

place

Hospital, southeastern Turkey

time

Present

• • •

[*In shadow two figures drag a 14-year-old girl* [YALOVA] *harshly by her hands and feet. These figures are played by* PERI *and* LATIFE, *but should be only dark shadows.*]

YALOVA   He came at night! In the thick dark black, I always saw him eyeing me. When I went to get the water. Bashed me down. Mud in my mouth. But something worse. So much worse!

[*The figures hurl* YALOVA, *who is now in rushing water.*]

Down there! Tumbling. Her inside me. Myself inside. That's all I can imagine. Too small. For this. Still playing games. With sticks. In the dark night. When he comes. Still playing games at night. Till my mother calls me, "Yalova, to bed! My little [*Screaming.*] Yalovaaaa."

[*Lights up on a hospital room.* YALOVA'*s mother,* PERI, *wearing a head scarf, is trying to drag* YALOVA *out of the room.*]

PERI   Yalovaaaa! My little one. Hurry!

[YALOVA *is bandaged, severely hurt.*]

YALOVA   Mama, they heard me crying. Down the river. The villagers came on their own. I did not call to them!

PERI   I myself will take you to the police.

YALOVA   I didn't tell the doctor, not yet, I promise . . .

PERI   Quiet, you will tell them your brothers had nothing to do with it!

YALOVA   But rocks . . . I bumped into rocks . . . Did it hurt her?

PERI   That's enough! What good are you to us now?

[LATIFE, *a Westernized woman, rushes into the room.*]

LATIFE   What are you doing to her? Get her back into that bed! Are you crazy?

PERI   This is not for you. There are certain things between a mother and daughter that are private.

LATIFE   Put her back in bed or I will get the police. Your sons left her for dead in that canal, Mrs. Bey.

PERI   She dishonored our family.

[LATIFE *struggles with* PERI *to get the girl* YALOVA *back into bed.* LATIFE *speaks to* YALOVA.]

LATIFE   Your two brothers are in jail. And your father, for ordering your killing.

YALOVA   Jail? No. Mama! I'm so sorry!

[PERI *changes tactics, helping* YALOVA *into the bed.*]

PERI   Now, now, hush, let me touch you. Does it hurt?

YALOVA   [*Softly.*] . . . Does it hurt her, Mama?

PERI   Shh-shh, lie still, little one. [*To* LATIFE.] We must pray now. Would you please leave us alone to pray?

LATIFE   I will be just outside the door.

PERI   May I ask you for a small favor? She needs cold water. Would you bring us some? She is ill and my own throat is parched, I have walked so far in the hot sun, my village is very far away . . .

LATIFE   I will need to speak to her. Do you understand?

PERI   The water. Please. You are very gracious, we are both unwell, please . . .

LATIFE   I'll get water.

[LATIFE *exits.* PERI *whispers to* YALOVA *so* LATIFE *won't hear.*]

PERI   What have you done? Are you mad?

   [*Shaking her.*]

   Stupid foolish child!

YALOVA   They are not really in jail, Mama?

PERI   You went to the police. To shame us! You must go back now and say it was a story you invented. It is you who jumped into the canal to save yourself.

YALOVA ...But he came, the neighbor. In the night. I was playing alone...Mama...

PERI And what is inside you now? Bad, bad girl!

[PERI *starts to hit her.*]

YALOVA Stop, Mama. I keep thinking why didn't you call me to bed a little earlier that night...

[*Calling like her mother.*] "Yalovaa..."

[PERI *yanks* YALOVA *back out of the bed.*]

PERI On the road we will ask for help...

YALOVA My head, it is turning...

PERI I, who fed you, sang to you when you cried...

YALOVA ...turning...

PERI What are you worth to us now?

YALOVA The walls slipping...

PERI We can get no money for you!

YALOVA What will you do to me?

[YALOVA *slips to the floor.*]

Don't kick me, Mama. [*Shielding her stomach.*] Be careful...

PERI I will kill you right here! Then you will see what a curse you have brought on this family. I, all alone, without our men. I SAY GET UP AND WALK.

YALOVA   STOP IT, PLEASE!

[LATIFE *reenters with a pitcher and glass of water.*]

LATIFE   [*Furious.*] Get away from her. Move away from her.

PERI   Let go of me.

[PERI *starts to hit* LATIFE.]

LATIFE   Move away from her, stop it!

PERI   I am her mother.

LATIFE   Mother? Kicking her like that.

PERI   What would you know of it?

LATIFE   Move away. [*Throwing water on* PERI.] Now sit in that chair and stay until I am finished.

PERI   I will stand.

LATIFE   Move away from her.

PERI   I will stand.

LATIFE   Stand at a distance.

PERI   Give me some water.

　　　[LATIFE *fills the glass and hands it to her.*]

　　　Give her some water.

[LATIFE *kneels next to* YALOVA.]

LATIFE   Can you hear me?

[PERI *starts to approach* YALOVA *again.*]

Don't you come closer, go back to the chair.

PERI   She needs a doctor.

[LATIFE *whispers to* YALOVA.]

LATIFE   You did well to survive—thrown into an irrigation ditch. You floated at least a mile down the canal.

[YALOVA *whimpers.*]

[*Comfortingly.*] Shh-shh. The villagers that rescued you said your cries were so loud, like an animal's. Like an animal they could not recognize. It was not your fault, you did well to tell the police. Right after they threw you in your brothers shot your neighbor... the man who raped you. Your brothers hoped to kill you too... No mind can wrap itself around such a thought.

PERI   She is with child. [*Motioning to* YALOVA's *stomach.*] That is what happened.

[LATIFE *looks at* PERI, *then at* YALOVA.]

LATIFE   [*To* YALOVA.] Really?

[YALOVA *nods.*]

PERI   Stupid girl.

LATIFE   Come, let me help you back into the bed, we need to call the doctor.

[YALOVA *hallucinates.*]

YALOVA   In the rain time there was silver on the canal.

LATIFE   Stand up, now, that's good.

YALOVA   Like a million fish.

LATIFE   One foot in front of the other.

YALOVA   Sun so bright on the silver, like blinding lights...

LATIFE   Almost there, you'll rest...

YALOVA   Don't go in the water, it's dirty, Mama told us...How could something so beautiful be so dirty, just put a foot in, a toe...

LATIFE   Let me put the blanket around you. You're not the only one, by far, but when the girl dies the crime disappears. Not with you, Yalova. Not with you.

YALOVA   How could something so beautiful be so dirty?

[PERI *gets up from the chair.*]

PERI   My water is finished. [*Obsequious.*] I must approach, lady. If it is not asking too much. [*To* YALOVA.] You will go to the police and tell them your brothers and father are not to blame. To restore their honor.

LATIFE   And hers?

PERI   It is not for her to have.

LATIFE   Sometimes I ask myself, did I really come from this country?

PERI [*Disgusted.*] You left.

LATIFE No, I live here, in Istanbul. I've been here all my life.

PERI Istanbul!

[LATIFE *faces* PERI.]

LATIFE I will protect her now.

PERI And our family? Will you protect us? Without a husband and sons I will become so poor I will survive on handfuls of dirt. All my village: "There goes the dishonored one."

[*She spits on* YALOVA.]

Rotten girl.

YALOVA [*Faintly.*] Mama...

PERI Don't call to me now.

YALOVA If only you'd called...

PERI Too late, you should have come with me before when I told you to.

YALOVA If only you'd called me a little earlier to bed that night. [*Imitating her mother, calling.*] "Yalovaa!"

PERI Nonsense! You know what you must do to save us.

[PERI *puts her scarf over her head and exits, head bowed against the hot sun ahead.* LATIFE *stands a moment, then approaches the hospital bed.*]

LATIFE My name's Latife Inan.

[*She stands looking at* YALOVA, *who curls into herself.*]

There are other girls. Perhaps in your village you heard rumors... A girl who died because she brought dishonor on her husband, not getting permission to go to the movies. Another's throat cut because a love song was dedicated to her on the radio.

I will return to the city to prepare your case. We'll place you under security protection. We'll send you somewhere where you'll be safe. When you're better you must agree to testify.

Let me get the doctor...

[LATIFE *starts to go.* YALOVA *whimpers.* LATIFE *sees a little girl, in pain, with a baby inside her.*]

When I was a little girl my own mother died. She died in a car crash—if you ever go to Istanbul, you'll see that traffic lights are only there for decoration. They say my mother was the type to stop at them. So... I was raised by men. My father, two brothers taught me how to excel, study hard, debate at the dinner table, defend my honor. I went to the best university, was lauded by my teachers, lauded especially by my father and my brothers, who always seemed giddy that I, a woman, their creation, succeeded so well, worked out so right.

[LATIFE *speaks with self-deprecation.*]

Now I am a senior lawyer, but there is no place to debate at the dinner table about people like you. Your fate is unthinkable to those who raised me. These men would never understand how in your belly will be your life, yourself; how that woman who walked out the door is still your heroine; how the canal you traveled down is both your road to freedom and the rope to hang you. That silvery mirage you speak of, just out of reach . . . I will fight with what I have been given by those men who honor me so highly. For them it's all for common markets, but that's not what it is for me. I will have to fight this their way, the way my own father taught me, for you, Yalova. Now let me go get the doctor.

[*Back to the rushing canal.*]

YALOVA   And I was in it. Swirling. Diving. Gasping. I was in the canal. More than my toe. But my whole body. I screamed not for me. Because I would rather have drowned than dishonor my mother, My father, my brothers. Whom I loved so much. But I screamed. For her . . .

[*She is holding a baby in her arms. It is in the future.*]

The girl I chose to call Latife. Born into a world of men.

• • •

Brown

Cherie Vogelstein

Cherie Vogelstein

Cherie Vogelstein's plays have been produced Off-Broadway, Off-Off-Broadway, and all over the world.* A favorite among college students, Vogelstein's one-acts have received over 200 university and amateur productions throughout the United States. Shortly after being awarded Best Emerging Playwright of 2000, Cherie's one-act *Cats and Dogs* took the Jury Prize at the HBO Arts Festival and was made into a short film. Feeling, however, unable to achieve the fame and glory of her Nobel Prize–nominated oldest brother, or her Pulitzer Prize–winning brother-in-law, or her *Dora the Explorer*–creator husband, Cherie has chosen to devote all of her energies to her three children. She currently lives in Manhattan, waiting for divine intervention.

*Special thanks to the Ensemble Studio Theatre and Curt Dempster.

• • •

[*Interviewer,* IRA BURKE, *a most congenial, father-figure type, sits at wide, wooden desk, in sumptuous executive office suite. Younger applicant,* PETER TELKE, *an earnest, sincere Ivy Leaguer, sits across from him.* PETER *wants this job, very much. Note: There should be NO pauses in dialogue except where noted.*]

PETER   About eighteen months?

IRA   [*Looking at papers.*] Eighteen months.

PETER   Oh, well, I got—I got sick for a little while in there—

IRA   Oh, I'm sorry. [*Beat.*] What, uh...what was wrong? If I may...?

PETER   Well, it's kind of...complicated.

   [IRA *waits.*]

   Okay: First I had a...burst appendix—

IRA   Oh no—

PETER   And then, in the hospital, I contracted pneumonia.

IRA   [*Sympathetic.*] Geez!

PETER   Yeah, so it kind set me back for a while, laid me up for close to three months.

IRA   Three months! Wow, a young kid like you.

PETER   Yeah, it was, it was kind of a hard time—

IRA   I'll bet, I'll bet, with your kind of drive. [*Looks at papers.*] And your parents?

PETER   My parents?

IRA   Ya know, were they, uh...were they supportive during that period?

PETER   Oh, well, it's just my mother now. My father passed away last year.

IRA   I'm so sorry.

PETER   Thank you. Thanks. Well, but...life has to go on, right? [*Beat.*] I'm ready to work hard!

IRA   [*Smiles genuinely.*] Good, good. [*Beat.*] So! It says here Artie Winslow was your D.M.—

PETER   Yes. Yes, he was.

IRA   I know Artie well.

PETER   Oh!

IRA   How'd you, how'd ya get along with him?

PETER   With Artie?

IRA   Right.

PETER   Well, um...ya know, pretty good. We—we didn't exactly...see eye to eye on every, single...project, but, for the most part, I'd say pretty good. Good.

IRA   Like what?

PETER   Um...?

IRA   What didn't you see eye to eye on? What projects?

PETER   Oh. Well . . . let's see: ya know, the applications systems for KM3s? Are you familiar with—

IRA   Sure.

PETER   Well, we really—

IRA   He says here you had some "control issues."

PETER   He did? Well, I think . . . maybe he had some . . . resented my age.

IRA   [*Smiles broadly.*] Really? He's not such an old guy, is he?

PETER   No, no, but . . . he just, he was rooted to HIS . . . way of doing things, ya know? and I—I wanted to . . . deviate a little sometimes, from the standard—

IRA   [*Looking through papers.*] Interesting.

PETER   I mean, that's one of the reasons I left Dunlap actually, because I just, I wasn't finding it very stimulating. At all.

IRA   No?

PETER   I mean, the way I spent my time was . . . well, I wanted to be doing . . . MUCH more with my time.

IRA   And what *were* you doing? With your time.

PETER   Truthfully? I was browsing the Internet. A lot.

IRA   Love to browse the Internet.

PETER   I know, but I'd finish my work like around 11 a.m.?

IRA   11 a.m.?

PETER   And have the rest of the day to kill, so to speak. That's not—that's not—

IRA   [*Chuckles.*] Eleven o'clock! That's early!

PETER   I know! And I ... I really thrive on a challenge, ya know? [*Beat.*] I need to be challenged.

IRA   Do you.

PETER   That's why I was so ... I'm so, I'd ...

IRA   Hey! You want something to drink? [*Stands.*] Some tea or ...

PETER   [*Also stands.*] Oh no, no, thank you, I was just—[*Starts to sit.*]—I was gonna say—[*Sees* IRA *is still standing, pops back up immediately.* IRA *then turns, begins attending to tea service near desk.*]—the kind of really innovative ... complex undertakings going on HERE—

IRA   [*Back to him, at tea service.*] Right, right—

PETER   Just so exciting and ... I was, at Dunlap and Fritz, I was basically just ... killing time. [*Smiles sheepishly.*] I already said that.

IRA   [*Leans over intercom.*] Maurie? Can you come in here for a second?

[MAURIE *enters instantaneously. Walks with a major swagger—or is it a limp?*]

Maurie, this is Pete Telke—

PETER   [*Half-rises, shakes.*] Peter, Peter Telke, nice to meet you.

MAURIE   How ya doing?

IRA   [*To* MAURIE.] Can you sit? You have a few minutes?

MAURIE   Sure.

[*Sits, beat.*]

IRA   Pete was with Winslow at Dunlap and Fritz.

MAURIE   Oh yeah?

IRA   About eighteen months.

MAURIE   [*To* PETER.] Why'd you leave?

PETER   Dunlap and Fritz?

MAURIE   Yeah.

IRA   He was bored.

MAURIE   Nice.

IRA   [*Nods approvingly, to* MAURIE *about* PETER.] This kid . . .

MAURIE   [*Impressed.*] Oh yeah? [*Beat.*] So how'd ya like Winslow? Is he retarded or what?

PETER   [*Smiles shyly.*] Well . . .

MAURIE   [*Grabs* PETER'*s knee, playfully.*] Come on, you know what I'm sayin', YOU know what I'm sayin'!

IRA   [*Laughs.*] Artie's alright, he's . . . [*To* MAURIE.] Tea, Maurie?

MAURIE   Great. With honey, please. [*Beat.*] So, Pete. Where'd you go to school?

PETER   Oh, Brown.

MAURIE   Brown! [*To* IRA, *who is still fixing tea.*] Marshall went to Brown.

IRA   He did? I didn't know that.

MAURIE   Yep. [*Longer beat.*] Hey! you want me to call Mary in? [*To* PETER.] Mary's great!

IRA   Yeah, call Mary, would you?

MAURIE   [*Calls loudly.*] Mary!

IRA   [*To* PETER.] Mary's the—

[MARY *also enters instantaneously.*]

MAURIE   [*Loudly.*] Here she is! Mary, Mary—

MARY   Here she is, here she is. [*Looking around confidently.*] Hello, boys.

PETER   [*Stands.*] Peter Telke.

MAURIE   [*To* IRA, *jokingly.*] He didn't stand up for ME.

MARY   [*To* MAURIE, *looking at* PETER.] You're not Mary.

IRA   NO ONE is Mary.

MARY   [*Shaking* PETER's *hand; a supportive, mother figure.*] I'M not even Mary.

MAURIE   Mary was with the Rockettes.

MARY   [*Still holding his hand, smiling warmly.*] No, I wasn't.

MAURIE   Pete here went to Brown.

PETER   [*A whisper.*] Pe-Peter.

MARY   Oh, you went to Brown? [*To* IRA.] Marshall went to Brown. [*Softly, shakes her head sadly.*] Marshall.

IRA   Yeah, was he smart? I didn't think he was that smart.

MARY   Well, he went to Brown.

IRA   Go figure.

MAURIE   So, what'd you do at Brown? Any sports?

PETER   Um...

MAURIE   Lacrosse?

PETER   No...no.

MAURIE   [*Surprised.*] Really?

PETER   [*Beat, offering hopefully.*] I played badminton for a while.

MAURIE   Badminton?!

IRA   [*To* MARY.] Is that a sport?

MARY   It's a great sport! [*To* PETER.] I love badminton!

MAURIE   [*Laughing.*] You love badminton. [*To* PETER.] She never played badminton in her life.

MARY   [*Smiling.*] How do you know?

IRA   [*To* PETER, *amused.*] What do you think? Has she ever played badminton in her life?

PETER   Uh...I don't...know, I—

MAURIE [*Swats his knee playfully.*] Well, of course you don't
KNOW—

MARY [*Ignoring MAURIE.*] So you played badminton too, Peter?

PETER [*Quickly.*] Yeah, I got into it cuz my girlfriend—

IRA [*Relieved.*] Oh!

[*Vigorously erases note on paper.*]

PETER She—she played all the time. She was kind of addicted.

MAURIE Addicted to badminton?

MARY Like me.

MAURIE Yeah, right. [*Turns to face her fully.*] What equipment do
you use for badminton, Mary?

MARY What?

IRA [*To PETER, and aside.*] Watch this.

MAURIE What kind of equipment—

MARY Rackets!

MAURIE [*Winks at IRA.*] And what else?

MARY What else?

MAURIE Look at her stalling. She has no idea.

PETER [*To MARY, helpfully.*] You use a birdie.

MARY A birdie!

[PETER *smiles at her.*]

MAURIE   [*Severe, to* PETER.] Why did you tell her?

PETER   [*Hangs head.*] Oh.

IRA   Maurie played lacrosse at Johns Hopkins.

PETER   Did you?

MAURIE   [*Nice again.*] Yeah, I'm always looking for good players. Love to get a team going up here.

IRA   He's a total . . . lacrosse nut.

[PETER *nods, smiles, they all look at* PETER. *A long beat.*]

So, Peter. What . . . what excited you?

PETER   [*Slightly confused.*] Um . . . ?

IRA   If you could work on any—design your own projects, what would you—

PETER   Oh! Well—

MARY   [*Stands abruptly.*] I have to go!

MAURIE   Why?

MARY   I'm a little bored—

[*They laugh; to* PETER.]

No, actually, I have a conference call at 2:15.

IRA   Well, it's only 12—Peter?

PETER   Yes, um—

IRA   [*Serious.*] If you had to have sex with either your mother or a dog, who would you pick?

PETER   [*Smiling.*] Wh-what?

MARY   [*At the same time, sits.*] Oh, okay.

IRA   Which one...would you pick?

PETER   [*Confused smile.*] Um...?

MAURIE   Meaning, if you had to FUCK your mother. Or a dog—

IRA   Ya know, somebody comes over to you and says you HAVE to have intercourse—

MAURIE   Penetration—

IRA   Right, with either. A dog. Or your own mother—

MARY   What kind of a—

MAURIE   [*An aside to* MARY.] You love badminton.

IRA   What would you...

PETER   [*Half-laugh.*] I'm a...I'm a little confused—

MARY   You didn't tell him what KIND of dog, Ira—

MAURIE   A poodle. I hate fucking poodles.

IRA   [*Magnanimous.*] Any kinda dog you want. [*Beat.*] All right, a German shepherd. A German shepherd. Nice, cooperative dog.

MARY   I can't stand German shepherds.

MAURIE   That's not what I hear!

PETER   [*Half-smile.*] I don't...I don't get it.

IRA   What do you mean?

PETER   [*Same half-smile.*] Oh, well, I just...why...why would you ask me...?

MAURIE   [*Smirking, mock sensitivity.*] Is...this a sensitive area for you, Pete?

PETER   [*Trying to laugh, shaking his head.*] I just...don't...

IRA   You've interviewed before, haven't you, Peter?

PETER   Oh, of course—

IRA   And that question's never come up?

[*They all laugh.*]

No, seriously, you can learn a lot about a person from a question like that.

PETER   Really?

MAURIE   Ask me, Ira!

IRA   All right, Maurie. Your mother or a dog.

MAURIE   A dog!

IRA   A dog! We have an answer! [*To* PETER, *happily.*] Ya see? He says a dog!

MARY   Ya know, you really are sick, both of you.

IRA   Not at all—

MAURIE   Okay, big talker, what about you?

MARY   What ABOUT me?

MAURIE   Your father or a dog.

MARY   Oh! My FATHER or a dog, that's different. [MARY *drinks from* MAURIE's *tea.*] Hmm.

IRA   A, uh . . . a Doberman for you, Mary.

MARY   Thank you, Ira, but I really don't care for Dobermans.

IRA   Oh, you don't? I didn't know that.

MAURIE   She very particular. She likes beagles.

MARY   I do, I love beagles. I have a beagle.

MAURIE   Do you fuck him?

MARY   [*To* PETER.] They're very sick.

MAURIE   [*To* PETER.] WE'RE sick. She fucks her pet beagle and WE'RE sick.

MARY   [*To* PETER.] I would never fuck Harry.

MAURIE   [*To* PETER.] Harry's her husband.

MARY   Harry's my beagle. [*To* MAURIE.] I would BLOW Harry but I would NEVER fuck him.

[*They laugh.*]

IRA   [*To* PETER, *explaining good-humoredly.*] Ya see, Peter, it's important to—

MARY   All right! My father.

MAURIE   [*Shocked.*] Your father?

IRA   Mary, Mary, mother of Christ, your father of all people.

MARY   Of course.

MAURIE   "Of course," yet!

IRA   Why "Of course," Mary?

MAURIE   So let's ask a different . . . : Your father or your HUSBAND?

MARY   Let me think.

[*They laugh.*]

IRA   [*To* PETER.] The ability to . . . laugh, joke around in a high-pressured environment—

[PETER *checks his watch.*]

MAURIE   Uh-oh, he's looking at his watch.

IRA   Are you in a rush, Peter?

PETER   No, I just . . . I actually—

MAURIE   No, but really, THAT'S—[*To* MARY.] "My father!" [*To* PETER.] Is that sick or what?

PETER   [*Half-smile.*] Well, this whole conversation's a little . . .

[*Silence, they all look at* PETER.]

IRA [*Sweetly.*] What? [*Beat.*] Look, Peter. I could ask you the
standard interview questions till kingdom come, but that
just not gonna give me a tenth of the—

MAURIE Excuse me, but I can't get over—[*To* MARY.] How could
you pick your father, Mary? That is so...

MARY [*To* PETER.] He's jealous.

MAURIE [*Laughing but serious.*] I'm serious! I mean, at least with a
dog, there's no... awkward moments afterwards, no...
memories—

MARY How do you know?

MAURIE If you see the dog on the holidays, it's not uncomfortable
for anybody.

MARY What if he remembers the smell of my crotch? What if he
attacks my crotch on the holidays? My father's not gonna
do that.

MAURIE [*Considers this.*] That's a good point.

IRA [*To* PETER, *tapping his temple.*] Ya see? Makes ya think. [*Beat.*]
So?

PETER [*Shaking his head.*] Um... I really... don't have an
answer—

MAURIE You don't?

[*Pause.*]

IRA   Well...say someone had a gun to your head and they told you to answer or they'd kill you—

PETER   Well, that would never happen.

MAURIE   [*Rolling his eyes.*] Theoretically.

PETER   But...I mean, why would anyone do that?

IRA   [*Pause, squinting at* PETER, *pencil to his lips.*] Do you want this position, Peter?

PETER   [*Trying to laugh it off.*] Of—of course I do! But do I—do I need to have sex with my mother or a dog to get it?

MARY   [*Laughing with relief.*] Ohhh, that's the problem! He thinks he has to actually DO it!

IRA   [*Laughing.*] Noooo!

MAURIE   It's a hypothetical!

PETER   I understand that—

MAURIE   Just pretend you're on the badminton court—slam that birdie back!

IRA   Team player kind of stuff.

PETER   Okay, okay, just...bear with me for a second: Under what circumstances would I ever, EVER have to make that choice?

IRA   You mean here at work?

PETER   Well, yeah...anywhere, really.

MARY Nazi Germany. Sophie's choice.

PETER No—

MARY What do you mean no? They had people making far
worse choices than that. I ought to know.

MAURIE Why should YOU know?

MARY [*Beat.*] My parents were survivors.

[*They guffaw.*]

PETER [*Horrified.*] You're laughing about survivors of the
Holocaust?!

MAURIE [*Still laughing.*] Here parents are *Irish*, for Christ's sake.

IRA [*Gently.*] Listen, Peter. You've been an overachiever all your
life, am I right?

PETER Well...

IRA Have some fun! Relax!

PETER [*To* IRA, *after a pause.*] Mr. Burke? [*Beat.*] I know Artie
Winslow said I have some control issues—

IRA This has nothin' to do with that—

PETER Well, maybe there's some truth to that in that... I mean,
I consider myself a very principled person—

IRA Okay—

MAURIE What does that mean?

PETER   Just that—

MAURIE   We're not principled?

PETER   No, no—

IRA   Peter, Peter. No one's asking you to violate your principles here—

MAURIE   But what does that mean, he's a very principled person. That feels like a judgment or something.

PETER   I didn't mean it that way at all—

IRA   How DID you mean it, son?

PETER   I just meant—

MARY   He wants to be his own man.

IRA   [*Nicely.*] Let him speak for himself, Mary.

PETER   I just...I have...my boundaries—

MAURIE   Yeah?

PETER   And, well, you have to admit...it's very offensive—

MAURIE   I'M not offended [*To* MARY.] Are you offended, Mary?

MARY   Well, it's a subjective kinda—he's not used to our kind of humor.

PETER   [*Hopefully.*] So—so is that it? Is it—is it some kind of an inside joke?

IRA   Well, it started out that way, but . . . to tell you the truth, I'd
      really like to know the answer now. [*He leans forward now,
      gentle but intense.*] Because I have to tell you, Peter Telke . . . I
      was really considering you for the position—AM really
      considering you—

MAURIE   He only calls me in when he's seriously interested in
      the candidate.

MARY   SERIOUSLY interested.

IRA   I asked you a simple albeit unorthodox question because I
      wanted to see how you'd respond—how you WILL
      respond. And by NOT responding—

MAURIE   Maybe he doesn't want the job!

PETER   What?! No!

MAURIE   Basically saying, "Fuck you guys. I don't need to answer
      your fucking asinine questions, I don't need your fucking
      job."

PETER   That's not at all what I'm saying—

IRA   So what exactly ARE you saying, Peter? Because this is
      important.

[*Pause.*]

PETER   I mean, for all I know you could want me NOT to
      answer, right? To test my . . .

      [MARY *shakes her head no;* PETER *thinks hard, sweating.*]

      But I mean this is just to see if I'm a "team player," really,
      right?

IRA You're in the big leagues now, Peter—this is not Dunlap and Fritz.

PETER No, I know, I understand that, believe me!

IRA [*Calmly.*] Look. No one wants this to turn ugly—

PETER Wh-what do you mean?

MARY [*Confidingly, to* PETER.] Well, it's almost like a slap in the face now, ya know? It's...

PETER Is it? I don't mean it to... but... it—it's really, it IS an obscene question, Mary, you see that.

MARY Of course!

PETER So to direct my mind to... ya know? Thoughts like that. I've worked hard to...

MAURIE To what?

PETER To... to *avoid* those thoughts.

IRA Peter. Peter. You're turning this into another power struggle, Peter—

PETER [*Torn.*] Am I? It's just that I don't want to waste my time on—

MARY But you're wasting much more time by NOT answering, don't you see?

PETER Yes, but... I—I just can't answer ANYTHING anybody asks me!

MAURIE Why not?! I feel like killing this guy!

IRA Calm down, calm down. [*Nods to* MARY.] Lock the door, Mary.

PETER [*Really scared.*] Lock the door?!

MARY [*Locks the door, muttering.*] This is...

IRA I don't want to be disturbed—[*Beat.*] Peter. What would it take to get you to answer this question?

PETER Why did you just lock the door?

IRA Department head? Would that do it? Because this is getting insulting.

PETER Department head?

IRA Theoretically.

PETER You're offering me—

IRA If you answer.

PETER If I answer this question, you're offering me head of the department of Research and Development?

MARY [*Rooting for him.*] Come on, Peter!

[PETER *thinks awhile.*]

MAURIE [*Explodes.*] Look, he's still—unbelievable!

PETER No, I want to. I... [*Beat.*] I'm sorry. I just...

MARY What?!

PETER I... can't do it. I can't answer a question like that, in good conscience. I can't!

MAURIE   He—he thinks he's renouncing his fucking religion, for Christ's fucking sake. [*To* PETER.] No one's asking you to KILL the fucking dog.

MARY   OR your mother—

IRA   Don't turn this into a point of honor, really—

MARY   It's just a question! A string of words!

PETER   Everything's a string of words, Mary, starting out as a theoretical question in someone's mind: If I do this to this person, to these people, to this country! what will happen?

IRA   You're losing perspective here!

PETER   [*To* MARY.] YOU brought up the Holocaust—

MARY   I did?

PETER   To—to entertain such a question—it's unethical!

MAURIE   Unethical?! WHAT?!

IRA   Unethical to answer, Peter, or unethical to think about it?

PETER   Well—well ... both. Both!

IRA   [*Very calm.*] Ya know, and this is what I was talking about before: Every day, every working day, you'll be confronted with choices, forced to prioritize—

PETER   I know! But—

MARY   Think Darwin!

MAURIE   It's ... what's enraging is—ya know? No matter what, he won't—

IRA You have to exercise common sense—you understand?

PETER Yes, I do! But—but ... you have to also be a person too, don't you?

MAURIE What the fuck is he talking about?

MARY I just wish—

MAURIE This is an INTERVIEW, this is a QUESTION—

IRA All right, all right. Peter, say you'd lose a finger—

PETER What?

IRA If you didn't answer, you'd lose a finger.

[PETER *looks at* MARY, *terrified.*]

PETER What are you saying to me?!

MARY [*Pleading, to* PETER.] You're being crazy!

PETER I'M being crazy?

MAURIE [*Takes out penknife.*] Which finger do you want to lose?

PETER I don't believe this.

IRA Theoretically, theoretically.

PETER I don't fucking believe this!

IRA You've brought this on yourself, my young friend. Making more of this than it is.

MAURIE Chu-rist!

[PETER *looks around room searchingly.*]

IRA   Why are you looking around?

PETER   Are we—is this some kind of a science experiment, a
    psychological test to—

IRA   It started out quite innocently.

MARY   If you would just answer—

MAURIE   You're a Nazi-boy, aren't you?

PETER   What?!

MAURIE   [*In Nazi accent.*] You have your principled orders—

[*Clicks his heels.*]

PETER   Mr. Burke!

MAURIE   But the principle is in your fucking head! [*To* IRA.]
    What'll he come up with tomorrow?

IRA   I mean, you've escalated this, Peter, you really have.

PETER   I?! [*Tries to get to door.*] Jesus!

MAURIE   [*Blocking his way, imitating Nazi.*] "I vill not use
    Microsoft. I am a very principled person."

[*Does Nazi salute.*]

IRA   [*Looking at papers.*] Turned it into a power struggle. You did.

MAURIE   Winslow was right.

PETER   [*To* MARY.] Please, please!

MARY [*Tenderly.*] Peter. Listen to me. I'm not a bad person. I'm telling you to answer, or it's your fault.

PETER What if—what if I start screaming?

IRA This is a sound-proof office.

MAURIE Only pussies scream.

PETER I'm having a déjà vu, have I see this in a movie? Am I in a movie, am I dreaming?

MAURIE You'll know after I cut off your finger.

PETER Is it because I wanted this job too much? Is God—

IRA Having principles is one thing. This is a self-aggrandizing—

MARY If you see a person drowning, you throw him a rope and he refuses to take it—you get angry, Peter! Just say it's your mother, all right?

PETER No. NO!

MAURIE The dog then!

PETER No! Fuck you!

[MAURIE *wrestles him down, cuts off tip of his pinky.*]

Oh my God! Oh my fucking God!

MARY Just pick one, pick one, PLEASE!

MAURIE You arrogant little JEW-boy—

IRA [*Overlap, with disgust.*] Come on, Maurie, don't do that— [*Looks at papers.*] And he's not Jewish—

PETER   OH MY JESUS! FINGER! I TYPE WITH MY
FINGERS! OH MY JESUS GOD!

MARY   He's right!

IRA   What?

MARY   Alfred Hitchcock did a movie with the fingers being cut
off.

IRA   Really?

MARY   Or was it Stephen King?

PETER   [*Wailing.*] I'm gonna die, I'm gonna die in here! [*To*
MARY.] Am I? Am I gonna die in this room?

IRA   What do you think?

PETER   [*To* IRA.] Like Marshall? Is this what you did to Marshall?
[*To* MAURIE.] YOU SICK ANIMAL-FUCKING,
MOTHERFUCKING BEASTS—YOU'RE GONNA
KILL ME!

MARY   [*Upset.*] You wanna die, Peter.

PETER   No, I don't! I don't want to die, Mary! I want to—

IRA   You don't have a death wish?

PETER   No, no, I want to live! I wanted a job! To live, to work!

IRA   Pride goeth before the fall!

PETER   [*Holding his ears.*] WORDS! Your filthy words killing
me—I AM A HUMAN BEING. I AM NOT A GAME.
JUST BECAUSE YOU SAY—

MARY   [*Suddenly pulling out switchblade.*] Answer or I'll take this razor and slash your wrists the way you want to do every time you take a bath.

PETER   I don't want to slash my wrists, I don't want to die—

IRA   Three people who obviously mean business. Are telling you, you might die. If you don't answer a simple question. And yet you refuse. Now you tell me you don't have a death wish.

[PETER *spits at* IRA.]

MAURIE   Did he just spit at you?

IRA   [*Calmly.*] Yes, he did.

[*Takes gun from desk drawer.*]

MARY   What is WRONG with you, Peter?! This is not a WESTERN!

PETER   YOU'RE the worst one.

MARY   [*Shocked.*] I'M the worst one?

MAURIE   [*Taking gun from* IRA.] Okay, that's it—

MARY   [*Holding him back.*] Wait— [*To* PETER.] How am I the worst one?

[*No response.*]

IRA   Mary asked you a question.

[PETER *starts to cry.*]

MAURIE   Is he crying?

MARY   How am I the worst one? I have been the only kind one in this room.

MAURIE   He hates his mother. You remind him of his mother.

MARY   Is that it? Do I remind you of the mother you want to fuck?

IRA   You are NOT scoring points for this—

[*Nods to* MAURIE, *who puts gun to* PETER's *bowed head.*]

PETER   When I saw the black pigeons—

MARY   Now I WANT them to kill you.

PETER   Is that what's meant for me? Is that what's gonna happen no matter what I would've said today, I was gonna die? Right? Wasn't I? Wasn't I? Wasn't I?!

[IRA *shrugs.*]

ANSWER ME!

IRA   You first.

PETER   [*Collapsing.*] My mother, all right? My mother! [*Sobbing softly.*] I would fuck my fucking mother.

[*Pause.*]

MARY   Now, was that so hard?

MAURIE   [*Grinning with relief.*] Je-sus Christ!

MARY   Whew!

IRA   He's a tough nut, all right!

MAURIE   [*Clapping him on the back.*] Three months in the loony bin, huh?

PETER   H-how did you . . . know about—

MAURIE   Hey . . .

MARY   It's all right, it's fine, Peter—

IRA   Ya see, in the end . . .

MAURIE   Ya just, ya gotta cut through the bullshit—

IRA   . . . It's all about posturing—

MAURIE   Gotta know who you are—

IRA   Knowing your limitations—

MARY   It really is—

IRA   As a means to realizing your potential.

MARY   It's an irony really.

[*Pause.*]

IRA   Unlock the door, Maurie, would you?

MAURIE   Sure. [*Off floor, hands it over.*] Hey, here's your pinky tip, Pete.

PETER   [*Uncertainly.*] Th-thank you. [*To* IRA.] Thank you.

IRA   So, Peter Telke. You think you can handle the job?

PETER   You mean...?

MARY   Congratulations, Peter.

PETER   You mean...?

MAURIE   [*Slaps his back.*] You're a Pane-Luger man now, Telke.

IRA   [*Chuckling.*] Almost, almost. [*Speaks into intercom.*] Anytime you're ready, Lo. [*To* PETER.] Just one more person I need you to—

MARY   Don't worry, this is just a formality.

MAURIE   She's gonna love ya!

[*They all laugh.* PETER *begins to relax, laughs with them.*]

PETER   So it was just a...a hazing, a—?

IRA   LIFE—[*A knock on the door.*]—it's open!—is a hazing. Wouldn't you say?

[*Door opens.*]

PETER   [*Horrified.*] Jesus God. Jesus God.

IRA   [*Rises graciously.*] Come in, Mrs. Telke. Come in.

• • •

and everybody else

Scott Organ

Scott Organ

Scott Organ is from Virginia and lives in Brooklyn, New York. His short plays *China* and *The Mulligan* were published in *New American Short Plays 2005*, edited by Craig Lucas, and have been performed throughout the country. His one-act plays *and everybody else*, *True North*, *Break Room*, *Runners*, and *The Mulligan* have been performed at Atlantic Theater Company's 453 New Works Series, a series he helped create. His full-length play *Fixed* premiered at the Hangar Theater in Ithaca, New York, and other full-lengths *The Faithful*, *City*, and *The Cold New* produced and/or workshopped in New York, Los Angeles, and Washington, D.C. He is also the author of the screenplay *Ghostkeepers* and the television pilot *The Program*.

• • •

[*A yard, outside a party.* DAVE *and* JANE.]

DAVE It was just like now. A party inside. Me out in the yard. Like we are now.

JANE Yeah?

DAVE And everybody else, they're indoors, they're still at the party, you know, I can see them on the front porch, and meanwhile this sweet little dog in the street appears to be dying.

JANE No.

DAVE Oh yeah. There was blood coming from its nose and ears.

JANE Oh God.

DAVE I mean, I thought it was over then. Blood from the ears?

JANE Sure.

DAVE Yeah.

JANE What did you do?

DAVE I stood out there—I tried to comfort it. I tried to help it.

JANE That was good of you.

DAVE But I didn't know what to do.

JANE That's so horrible.

DAVE I know.

[*Pause.*]

JANE So what happened?

DAVE Well. The dog is okay. You know. I heard it had surgery and now it's okay.

JANE Really?

DAVE Yeah. That's what I heard.

[*Pause.*]

But what I was struck by, you know, the thing I remember is the juxtaposition, you know, of the people at the party, the happy people and this dying little dog.

JANE Which did not die.

DAVE Well, right. Thank God. Yeah.

[*Pause.*]

My point being, and this is what struck me, that life is this strange ... It's this ...

JANE I agree.

DAVE You do?

JANE Oh yeah. Today at work.

DAVE Uh-huh.

JANE There was this delivery guy, this, uh, messenger.

DAVE Yeah?

JANE   Who was very strange.

DAVE   Really?

JANE   Yeah. It was...

[*Pause.*]

DAVE   Like how?

JANE   I don't know. I can't really...Just trust me on this, I know whereof you speak.

DAVE   Sure, good.

JANE   You should've seen this guy.

DAVE   I believe it. People do the strangest things.

JANE   They do.

DAVE   You know, in the end, I believe, we are all just animals.

JANE   I agree with that.

DAVE   No, hear me out.

JANE   I agree.

DAVE   Yeah, I know. It's true, isn't it?

JANE   Absolutely.

DAVE   We may pretend otherwise, but we are animals, just, you know, wandering around sniffing each other, spraying on trees.

JANE   Did you say spraying on trees?

DAVE   Marking our territory.

JANE   Right.

DAVE   Just . . . still animals.

JANE   I think you're right.

DAVE   You're a female, I'm a male.

JANE   I couldn't argue with that.

DAVE   You'd be a fool to try.

[*They laugh, pause.*]

What are you gonna do?

JANE   I don't know. What are you gonna do?

DAVE   No. I mean. I meant that rhetorically.

JANE   Oh.

DAVE   Sorry.

JANE   No. It's okay.

DAVE   I meant: what're you gonna do? The world. In all its bloodlust and baby killing, baby raping, religious nuts out there. Kids with guns.

JANE   Yeah, it's truly something else.

DAVE   They say, "think about this shit or the other," they say, "be upset and change and recycle."

JANE Yeah.

DAVE And my question therefore is what the hell are you gonna do?

JANE Yep.

DAVE Am I some sorta selfish bastard cause I wanna communicate with some, you know, lovely woman? Or have a couple of beers.

JANE I don't think so.

DAVE They wanna make me think I am. People in the news, on PBS, whatever...

JANE You can't believe everything you hear.

DAVE God no. God no, that is so true.

JANE We think that we're civilized people because we got e-mail but I tell you, remember those people in the Balkans or wherever that was—I tell you what. They wore Levis. They drank Dr Pepper.

DAVE And people in Africa, there are just tons of people over there still who go around and hack off people's limbs with machetes.

JANE Still?

DAVE I'm telling you they go around and hack off limbs. Like little baby limbs too. Some little girl, hacking off all these cute little girl's limbs.

JANE Her limbs.

DAVE   Yeah. Which I guess is just the arms and legs.

JANE   Not the head I hope.

DAVE   I don't think the head is considered a limb.

JANE   That would make sense. Because then all the talk would be about decapitations.

DAVE   Exactly. I hadn't thought of that.

JANE   Cute little boys and girls.

DAVE   Yeah.

>   [*Pause.*]

>   It's a lot to take.

>   [*Pause.*]

>   Do you need to get back?

JANE   Back?

DAVE   To the party.

JANE   Do you need to get back?

DAVE   No.

[*Pause.*]

JANE   I want to confide something to you.

DAVE   Okay, good.

JANE   Sometimes. Sometimes I get very umm...subdued.

DAVE   Me too. How do you mean?

JANE   Umm, I get . . . We live this long life, you know . . .

DAVE   Not so long.

JANE   Well, yes, right. Depending on . . . But what do we ever learn?

DAVE   Yeah. How do you mean?

JANE   What do we learn? We make the same, the same stupid mistakes over and over. It's crazy.

DAVE   Yeah, it is.

JANE   You're right.

DAVE   I am?

JANE   The world is hard.

DAVE   It is, I know.

JANE   The world is big. It's so big.

DAVE   I know.

JANE   And what I mean is, I get terribly lonely sometimes.

DAVE   Me too.

JANE   I'm not embarrassed to admit that. Terribly lonely. I cry. Sometimes I cry.

DAVE   I think that's good.

JANE   I do. I cry. About nothing at all. I cry during commercials. When the boy comes home for Christmas and makes coffee.

DAVE   Peter.

JANE   Yeah. The little girl, the sister, cries "Peter" when she sees him. Because no one thought he could come home. But he does. And I cry.

DAVE   I think you are so beautiful.

JANE   You do?

DAVE   I do. And right now. I feel very alive.

JANE   You do?

DAVE   I do.

JANE   What is your name again?

DAVE   Dave.

JANE   Dave. I want to do something.

DAVE   Me too. Like what?

JANE   I don't know. I don't . . . I want to rip off all my clothes and run down the street. With you.

DAVE   You do?

JANE   Through people's backyards. In people's backyards. Naked. Something.

DAVE   You do.

JANE   I do.

DAVE   Okay.

JANE   Did you see the guy in there? The guy with the olive coat, with the beard?

DAVE   Yeah.

JANE   That's my husband.

DAVE   Oh.

JANE   Yeah.

[*Pause.*]

DAVE   Yeah. My wife is in there.

JANE   Is she?

DAVE   Yeah. She's drunk, I think.

JANE   Which means, for all practical purposes, we should return.

DAVE   Yeah. I suppose we should.

JANE   You agree?

DAVE   With you?

JANE   Yeah.

DAVE   Do you?

JANE   Do I agree with myself?

DAVE   Yes.

[*Pause.*]

JANE   Say something to me.

DAVE   Say what?

JANE   Something, anything. I want you to say something to me.

DAVE   What do you want me to say?

[*Pause.*]

I think you're beautiful.

[*Pause.*]

JANE   Sometimes I just don't understand anything. And I'm not talking about the stock market or trigonometry. I'm talking about I don't understand not understanding. I don't understand a shower or breakfast. How I am supposed to behave. What happened to me as I got older. Nothing is ever like any story ever told. Nothing. Nothing is. Not with ten billion stupid things running amok in our heads. You know, that food tastes bad, or why can't I go to the bathroom this morning, or doesn't matter how often I clean the fucking tub, doesn't matter because life ultimately is only about one single solitary act, which is cleaning the tub over and over and over. So what? So we can clean ourselves. Who made the world like this? Who did? What I'm feeling now, what I'm feeling about ripping all my clothes off and running down the street, I'm very serious about this. Very fucking deadly serious. But do you know what? At some point, even if I held out till winter I would have to put my clothes back on. I would have to stop. I would have to clean the tub. What fools we are. What is

wrong with us out here? Are we so egomaniacal? Is that
what it is? Dave? Or whatever your name is.

DAVE   I just want to kiss you. That's all. There behind the trees.
Just kiss you. That's what I want to do.

JANE   Are you listening to me, Dave?

DAVE   Just kiss you some. Kiss your neck. Have you kiss me back.

JANE   Did you hear what I said?

DAVE   You want me to say something, I'm saying something.

JANE   What are you saying?

DAVE   I'm saying all I want is to kiss you. That's all I know now.
That's all I care about.

JANE   We kiss.

DAVE   Yes.

JANE   Close our eyes.

DAVE   Closed, opened, I don't care.

JANE   I would close my eyes.

DAVE   Okay.

JANE   But hurry.

DAVE   Yeah.

JANE   We've got to hurry.

• • •

Queenie

Murray Schisgal

Murray Schisgal

Murray Schisgal has an extensive career spanning plays, screenplays, fiction anthologies, and as a producer of five feature films. His Broadway plays include *Luv* (Tony nominated), *Jimmy Shine*, *All Over Town* (Drama Desk Award, Outstanding New Play), *The Chinese and Doctor Fish*, *Twice Around the Park*, and *An American Millionaire*. His films include *Tootsie* (Oscar nominated), *The Tiger Makes Out*, and *Luv* (based on the play).

Murray's Off-Broadway plays include *The Typists and the Tiger* (Vernon Rice Award, Outer Circle Award, Saturday Review Critics Poll Award), *Fragment*, *The Basement*, *The Flatulist*, *Walter*, *The Pushcart Peddlers*, *Sexaholics*, *Extensions*, *Road Show*, *Jealousy*, *Circus Life*, and *Angel Wings* (Off-Off-Broadway Award for Excellence).

Published works include *Days and Nights of a French Horn Player* (novel), *Luv and Other Plays* (collection), The Best American Short Plays series (twelve short plays over a number of years, published by Applause Books), and *Great American One-Act Plays*.

scene

A park bench on the east side of Central Park

time

Spring; Saturday, noon

• • •

[*At rise:* LAWRENCE ALBERTSON *enters, right, whistling cheerfully, perhaps the waltz from* Der Rosenkavalier.]

[*On a leash following him is* QUEENIE, *a smooth-haired fox terrier or a dog of similar size. Both owner and animal are groomed to a splendid shine.* LAWRENCE *is sixty-two years of age: he can easily pass for a man ten years younger. He wears a cashmere turtleneck sweater, an English hacking jacket, gabardine khaki slacks and cordovan jodhpurs; a pair of knit gloves dangle from his jacket's breast pocket. He passes the bench once, turns about, walks back to sit on bench. He beats the bench with his open hand.*]

LAWRENCE   Up here, Queenie! Up! Up, sweetheart! Up! Up!

[*Queenie jumps up on the bench. In the event that she doesn't respond to a specific command, the actor is given license to improvise whatever lines are necessary to accommodate her behavior; always, however, with shameless affection.*]

That's the girl. That's my good girl. You are the best. The best there is. Did I ever tell you how much I enjoy walking with you, huh? Did I? Did I? I can't imagine what I'd do with myself if you weren't around, my little friend.

[*He muzzles and pats* QUEENIE *on the rump.*]

The irony is that when I first saw you in the pet shop on Madison Avenue . . . Do you realize it was almost three years ago! Three years!

[*Reflectively.*]

Time. Time. Where does it go? Not the most scrupulous and attentive observation can alter . . . it's irrevocable momentum. Pity. Pity.

[*Said quickly.*]

Pity, pity, pity, pity.

[*Comes out of it.*]

Where was I? Oh, yes. Three years ago it was, when I first saw you. I hadn't the slightest intention of taking you home with me. I actually started walking away, heading down the street to Vito's. I did, I did, honest Injun! I don't know what got into me. Maybe it was the way you kept scratching at the window and making those shrill, yelping noises that sounded more like birds chirping than it did a dog barking. I made an abrupt about-face and I walked into the shop and once the sales boy placed you in my arms . . . I was sold. You were the cutest, cuddliest little creature I had ever seen in my entire life. I admit it. It was love at first sight, right from the start. I took you along with me into Vito's and showed you off to those Saturday afternoon martini drinkers and hangers-on. Afterwards I picked up my ready-to-go lunch of grilled calamari, pasta pomodoro and broccoli rabe, and I straightaway took you home.

[*He lifts* QUEENIE, *holds her in front of him.*]

Can you imagine the change you made in my life, huh? Can you? Can you? You were the first . . . living thing who shared my apartment with me in years; literally, literally in years. What a change it was. What a wonderful change. To get up in the morning to the sound of your playful barking,

your incessant jumping up and down on the bed, licking at
my face, pulling at the covers, not giving me a moment's
peace until I'm up and moving to the refrigerator to pour
you a bowlful of cold milk.

[*Laughing; scratching at* QUEENIE's *ear.*]

What a rascal you are. What a devil. Even after I've fed
you, you won't let me be until I've showered and dressed
sufficiently to take you out for your first walk of the day.
And how utterly rejuvenating it is, getting outdoors when
the air is still fresh and uncontaminated, the sun just
peeking above the horizon... One is glad to be alive...
that early in the morning.

[*Scans the sky.*]

One looks up at the luminous, infinite blue sky and
prays... without quite knowing why or to whom, feeling
quite silly about it and still... one prays, for another day
that brings to us... another early morning... with a
luminous, infinite blue sky.

[*To* QUEENIE.]

Oh, that is absolutely the best part of the day for me, those
early morning walks in the park with, when there's no one
about yet, except for an occasional pet lover like myself.

[LAWRENCE *acts out such a meeting. He puts* QUEENIE *back on the
bench beside him. He speaks to an imaginary passerby who is walking his
leashed, imaginary dog.*]

Good morning! Good morning! Lovely morning, isn't it?
That's a handsome Labrador you have there. I've noticed
him running...

[*Points to himself.*]

Mine? Queenie? You like her? You're taken with her intelligence? Her... Her lively disposition? Oh, she's an extraordinary companion. Absolutely extraordinary. You can't imagine the fun the two of us have together. We go everywhere. We...

[*Responds to an interruption.*]

Oh, yes, even when I'm out of town on a business trip. No exceptions to the rule. You don't leave your best friend alone in an apartment for any extended period of time. That's a no-brainer. My partners are well aware of my... Let's call them my prejudices.

[*He takes brush from his pocket and grooms* QUEENIE.]

I know this may sound strange to you, but perhaps you being a pet owner makes it possible for you to understand my feelings. I don't draw any distinctions whatsoever between a domestic pet and a human being. I am incapable of drawing such a distinction. I find it profoundly abhorrent to...

[*Responds to an interruption.*]

You'll get no argument from me there. The innumerable stories one hears and reads about: the sacrifices made by these domestic pets during fires, burglaries, physical assaults; the accounts of their unselfish devotion and bravery... There's a veritable library filled with such incidents. How any human being can think of being superior in any way whatso...

[*Responds to an interruption.*]

Vivisection? Did you say vivisection? Please, I implore you, don't get me started on that! The very word sends chills down my spine. If there's anything more heinous and unconscionable...

[*Responds to interruption.*]

I agree. Un-for-giv-able. Un-for-giv-able. We best move on to another...

[*Glances at wristwatch.*]

It is getting late. And I must be off. I have to pick up... Why, that is amazing. It is my birthday today. How in the world did you...?

[*Smiles broadly.*]

I guess with the Internet there's no having a private life nowadays. Thank you. Thank you. I appreciate the offer of a toast this evening, but I do have other plans. I'm sure I'll see you around again. Have a good day. Bye now. Bye...

[*He waves as the imaginary passerby moves off with his leashed dog. His hand falls to his lap. He continues grooming* QUEENIE; *solemnly.*]

Sixty-two, Queenie. Sixty-two. Gives one... food for thought. Pause for reflection. The paramount concern is: do I retire this year or wait until the big Six Five. I have to admit, I don't enjoy going into the office as much as I used to. The practice of law is no longer of any particular interest to me. All the old fellows are gone and all the new ones strike me as a greedy, uncivilized bunch. Not a gentleman among them. Not a one. Besides, think of all the time we'd have together if I retired. Wouldn't that be fun? Wouldn't you like that? Wouldn't...

[*A sigh.*]

> I can't believe it. Sixty-two. Sixty-two. Time. Time. Days. Weeks. Months. Years. Did I ever tell you I was once married? Did you know that, Queenie? I must have spoken to you about it.

[*A thoughtful beat.*]

> In any event, at the obscenely youthful age of twenty-four, soon after passing the bar exams, on my first try, you should know, I met a woman a year younger than myself through a client of mine.

[*As if searching for the correct pronunciation.*]

> Emma. Miss . . . Emma . . . Reynolds.

[*A beat.*]

> She was a social worker with the city, very much involved in child abuse cases. We dated, we . . . fell in love, we married and we moved into an apartment, a brownstone in Chelsea. We lived as fully and happily as any two young people possibly could.

[*As if searching for the correct pronunciation.*]

> Emma. Miss Emma Reynolds. Mrs. Emma . . . Reynolds . . . Albertson.

[*He removes a small plastic bag filled with dog biscuits from pocket; he feeds* QUEENIE.]

> I tell you, my little friend, our lives could not have proceeded more satisfactorily. I entered the field of

entertainment law and immediately found it both lucrative and challenging. Emma moved inexorably up the civil service ladder until she arrived at an administrative position of power and trust. And, I must say, for the five years of our marriage, there wasn't a day that passed that didn't have some special pleasure in store for us, whether it be a particularly outstanding dinner at a newly discovered bistro or, for no apparent reason and due to no deliberate design, an all-night entwining of blissful lovemaking.

[*A sigh.*]

Emma. My wife. My long-lost wife. Memories of what was; what could have been; what is not. She's remarried. With grown children now. Living...I know not where. Is she happy? I would think she is. The thrust of her being... always...Family. Values. Community.

[*A beat.*]

Emma. Miss Emma Reynolds. Mrs. Emma...Reynolds... Donleavy.

[*A desperate note.*]

You have to understand, Queenie, men and women, particularly, specifically, young men and young women... They are not the same. They do not desire the same things. They do not have the same goals and ambitions. You can argue, with some justification, that as they grow older, there is a coming together between the sexes, a joining of intentions and purposes and, ironically, even a physical sameness, as they are as babies, when they first come into this world. But not when they mature. Not when they are in the first full flush of their . . . sexual selves; the first full flush of their visceral, biological selves. Then they are decidedly different. Decidedly opposites. At odds. At loggerheads. There is no question about it. Absolutely no question about it.

[*Less emotionally.*]

Simply put, I was not in control of my own life. I was, in fact, under the control of . . . under the domination and beck and call of . . . an unrelenting sexuality. I was no more than an idiotic, weak-kneed, spineless puppet that was wagged heedlessly about on the strings of a mad puppeteer. That is the simple truth of it.

[*Meditatively.*]

Indeed it was. Indeed it was.

[*A beat.*]

Make no mistake about it, my dear friend, I had no control over my own life from my first year in high school until . . . until I woke up one morning in the recent past and suddenly realized that I had not fantasized an all-night entwining with some phantasmagoric lady love . . . in possibly weeks. It was at that particular point of time that I seemingly turned the corner from idiocy to sexual passivity and, once again, took control over my own life after a fifty-year hiatus.

[*A beat; aggressively.*]

As I said before, young men and young women are not the same, contrary to feminist propaganda. If a young woman confessed to being dominated by her libido as ruthlessly as I was, she would be deemed aberrant, afflicted with a pathological condition akin to nymphomania. But the reaction to such a confession from a young man would inevitably evoke a smile, a pat on the back and the gratuitous advice that he take a brisk, cold shower.

[*A beat.*]

And so it was with me. So it was, unrelentingly, incessantly. Even . . . Even when I was married to Emma.

Miss Emma Reynolds. Mrs. Emma . . . Reynolds . . . Donleavy.

[*A beat.*]

Even then, Queenie, even in the throes of my marital bliss, when I wanted for nothing, desired for nothing, loved dearly the woman I was living with . . . Even then my eye roved to catch a glimpse of an exposed thigh, a well-endowed breast, a pair of gracefully, insinuating buttocks, as my mind conjured sugar-plum scenarios of an all-night entwining with . . . another . . . another of unfamiliar scent, of unexplored texture, of unsuspected mysteries. Even then. Even then.

[*He takes a red ribbon from his pocket and makes a bow from it.*]

Still, no matter how helplessly I was lost in my adulterous fantasies, I observed, faithfully, the vows I had taken. Perhaps, if Emma had not introduced the thought of our moving to the suburbs, of our starting a family, buying a home, perhaps then, I would have observed the vows of our marriage for the remainder of my days. But once she had verbalized her deepest desires, her grand design for our common ... future, I ... I couldn't ... I couldn't relinquish my fantasies, nor free myself of this ... [*Stares down at his lap.*] distended abomination sulking between my legs.

[*He finishes knotting the red ribbon and ties it around* QUEENIE'*s neck.*]

Not then. Not at that time. Not at such a ... youthful age.

[*A beat.*]

I walked away, Queenie. Of my own volition, I left her. Over thirty years ago. I haven't seen her since. But I've heard from others about her health ... her interests ... her grown children, three of them, I'm told, and of an amiable husband ... who paints on weekends.

[*With vigor.*]

But don't you think for a second that I didn't fulfill every one of those ... of those fantasies of mine. Don't you think for a second I didn't have a ... a plethora of wildly gratifying and, yes, ecstatic times for myself. Let me tell you, my little friend, I wasn't in the entertainment business for nothing. The possibilities offered to me were limitless. I had over the years, more lovers of every conceivable size, shape, age, color, temperament and predilection than you can possibly imagine in a ... in a lifetime of Sundays!

[*Slaps his thigh.*]

Damn! I slept with tons of them! Lived with tons of them! Weeks. Months. Trips to Europe, the Far East, Africa, Alaska ... You name it and, word of honor, I did it! I had it! I left no bit of pulchritude untouched. No opportunity lost. No invitation ignored. No request denied!

[*Reflectively.*]

In the past, that is. In days gone, that is. Ages ago, it seems.
When I was wagged heedlessly about on the strings of a
mad puppeteer.

[*A sigh.*]

Yesterday's meal does not today's stomach fill. Every
morning one is hungry. Always hungry. Again. For
something. For anything.

[*He picks up* QUEENIE; *hugs her.*]

I'll tell you something, my little friend. It is my candid
opinion that I am presently in a position, emotionally in a
frame of mind, to entertain the prospect of a permanent
union.

[*Impatiently.*]

To put it simply, I'm quite ready to give marriage another
go-around. In fact, I've made a concerted effort recently to
meet eligible women of . . . mature years. I must say, I've
had enough of these young fly-by-nights. Frankly, they're
too insistent on their own pleasures for the likes of me. I
just don't have the patience for them anymore. I did start
dating, making inquiries, overtures. In good faith. Without
condition or prejudice. And yet . . . Maybe it's just a spell of
bad luck I've been having. So far I haven't been able to
connect, to find someone who is compatible, someone with
whom I can be . . . comfortable, like I was with Emma . . .
Miss Emma Reynolds. Mrs. Emma . . . Reynolds . . .
Donleavy.

[*Ruefully.*]

I guess there's no second-guessing who we meet, when we meet, how we meet. Statistically, the odds are heavily against us ever finding someone with whom we're comfortable with.

[*He's lost in reverie for a beat before shaking himself to movement.*]

But enough of this! Let's be off!

[*He rises, leash in hand, as* QUEENIE *jumps off the bench. With his free hand, he brushes off his slacks.*]

We'll pick up our lunch at Vito's: grilled calamari, pasta pomodoro and broccoli rabe for me; a nice osso bucco meat bone for you. And, oh, yes, if I forget you must remind me: a chilled bottle of sauvignon blanc.

[*He moves off, left.*]

After all, today is my birthday. We have to celebrate the occasion. In style. [*Pulling on leash.*] Come along, Queenie. Come along, sweetheart.

[*And they exit, with* LAWRENCE *singing to himself, "Happy birthday to me...Happy birthday to me...," using the name "Larry" in the appropriate line, as he exits stage with* QUEENIE.]

[*Lights fade out.*]

• • •

Reunions

Billy Aronson

Billy Aronson

Billy Aronson's plays have been produced by Playwrights Horizons, Ensemble Studio Theatre, Woolly Mammoth Theatre, and Wellfleet Harbor Actors Theater, published in *Best American Short Plays 1992–1993* and *1999–2000, Plays from the Woolly Mammoth, Best Stage Scenes 2003*, and *Ten Minute Plays from Actors Theatre of Louisville*, published individually by Playscripts, Inc., and awarded a New York Foundation for the Arts grant. His writing for TV includes *Courage the Cowardly Dog, Beavis & Butt-head, Wonder Pets, Upside Down Show, Backyardigans, Johnny and the Sprites*, and *Postcards from Buster* (Emmy nomination). His writing for the musical theater includes the original concept/additional lyrics for the Broadway musical *Rent. Reunions* was originally produced in Ensemble Studio Theater Marathon 2002, starring Hope Chernov, Katherine Leask, Thomas Lyons, Grant Shaud, and Maria Gabriele, directed by Jamie Richards. Visit www.BillyAronson.com.

characters

TABBY ECKERSLY is an independent publisher.

SARAH BURK NELSON is a mother.

ALAN ROADS doesn't know what he is.

RICK ARZOOMANIAN is a pirate.

NANCY MCCANN is a giraffe.

CONNIE CUMMINGS is Santa Claus.

BRANDON TAVELLE is a warlock.

• • •

[TABBY, SARAH, *and* ALAN *stand there talking (private).*]

TABBY   Because in publishing the manuscript is everything, if you don't like the manuscript, I mean, that's all you've got, it's your life.

SARAH   Sure.

TABBY   And I was getting manuscripts that, well, some of them were fine but I couldn't get behind them, not with every bone in my body.

SARAH   Uh-huh.

TABBY   And then one day I just woke up and it was clear as day that I had to just go ahead on my own.

SARAH   You're your own boss, that's so great.

TABBY   I have complete control, every single manuscript I believe in with every bone in my body, every fiber.

ALAN   I taught high school for eleven years! Then I quit and sold computers! Now I'm back in graduate school!

SARAH   I can't believe it's been nine years since I had a job.

TABBY   But you're a mom. That's so great.

SARAH   It's amazing, watching them figure stuff out, you learn so much.

TABBY   That's what everybody says.

SARAH   They're born with these real personalities, then they grow into these people that you really like, they're your pals, this whole team just came out of your body.

TABBY   It must be amazing.

SARAH   They can get you so angry, you never knew you could be so angry, or so in love, in whole new ways.

TABBY   I've really got to do that when I meet the right person.

SARAH   It's worth waiting for the right person.

ALAN   I keep meeting the right person but I can never convince her that I'm the right person!

TABBY   Now that I'm in control of my work it'll be easier.

ALAN   Let's head to the tent! There's going to be dancing!

SARAH   If I leave Bob with the kids one more minute, he'll kill me.

TABBY   Has anybody seen Donna Cunningham? We said we'd share a table.

SARAH   Did you hear Connie Cummings is going to be here?

TABBY   Connie Cummings, really? I can't believe it.

SARAH My kids are dying to meet her.

TABBY When I tell people I went to school with Connie Cummings they think I'm making it up. Hey, is that Rick Arzoomanian? [*To off.*] Rick. Rick.

[RICK *enters. He's a pirate.*]

TABBY Tabby Eckersly. Remember?

RICK Hey, Tabby.

TABBY Did you know Sarah Burk?

SARAH Sarah Burk Nelson.

RICK Sarah, sure.

ALAN I'm Alan Roads! I was friends with Gary Fine!

RICK Hey, Alan.

TABBY I read that you were a pirate in the paper, that's so great.

SARAH Really.

RICK I was getting nowhere on land. Just knocking on doors, year after year. So I put together a crew and headed out to sea.

TABBY You just did it.

SARAH That's so great.

RICK It was tough out there for a while. There was nothing happening and the sun was killing us.

TABBY Sure.

RICK   But then I saw this ship and I felt that it was ready for new ownership.

TABBY   You just had a feeling.

RICK   I felt the time was right and this was my chance. So I set my sights and I went for it with everything I had.

TABBY   Wow.

SARAH   I read about this.

RICK   It was a real battle, it was tougher than I thought. It cost me this eye, but we kept on fighting and we did it.

TABBY   That's something.

RICK   We pulled a real coup, and when I opened the treasure there were rubies and sapphires and diamonds packed together so tight. And just like that we went from struggling to stay afloat to being a major player on the sea.

TABBY   I'd been reading manuscripts that meant nothing to me, well, some were okay but I couldn't get behind them, so one morning I just woke up and decided to go independent and now it's great.

SARAH   I've missed working but you can't believe the way kids are born with these real personalities, you've got this whole team of people you love.

ALAN   I got sick of teaching, so I went into sales and now I'm back in school!

RICK   Has anyone seen Chris Dumars?

SARAH   Are you in touch with Chris?

RICK   I haven't seen Dumars in years.

TABBY   Did you hear Connie Cummings is going to be here?

RICK   I heard she might.

ALAN   Let's head to the tent for the dancing!

TABBY   I was going to wait for Donna Cunningham and get a table.

SARAH   I've really got to get back to Bob and the kids or he'll kill me.

[SARAH *goes.*]

TABBY   But to have all that treasure, right at your feet, all of a sudden.

RICK   I felt shocked, and I felt proud.

TABBY   Now that I'm finally working on manuscripts I really believe in it's so liberating.

RICK   There were emeralds and sapphires and rubies—

ALAN   Guess I'll head to the tent!

[ALAN *goes.*]

TABBY   And didn't it totally make up for all the years, you know, all the knocking on doors?

RICK   I had this feeling for the first time that I really was a pirate. I wasn't just pretending or going through the motions.

TABBY   At first I'd look down at these manuscripts and I couldn't believe I'm really attached to such brave and honest material that I can totally pour myself into.

RICK   We're a major player and heat isn't a problem, and we don't have to worry about the wind.

TABBY   My brain isn't chained to this garbage that I can't really get behind, I kept telling myself it would happen but it really has happened.

RICK   And I feel like this is just where I should be right now. And I'm headed exactly where I should be headed.

TABBY   Donna Cunningham's supposed to be here, we're going to get a table, you should join us.

RICK   That would be good.

TABBY   [*To off.*] Donna, is that you? Donna.

[NANCY *enters. She's a giraffe.*]

TABBY   Nancy McCann. I'm sorry. I thought that you were Donna Cunningham.

RICK   Nancy. Hi.

TABBY   So you're a giraffe.

NANCY   Yes.

[RICK *and* TABBY *look at* NANCY. NANCY *looks at them.*]

RICK   That's Donna Cunningham over there.

TABBY   [*To off.*] Donna, it's me, Tabby. Do you have an extra seat for Rick Arzoomanian? [*To* RICK.] She has an extra seat, you should join us.

RICK   That would be good. Except . . . is that Rich Kravitz at her table?

TABBY   Rich Kravitz and Donna used to go out.

RICK   I don't feel like sitting yet.

TABBY   But wouldn't you have a lot to say to Rich since he's a pirate too?

RICK   I think I'll stay here.

TABBY   He's a really successful pirate, you know that, right, from the papers?

RICK   I don't read the papers.

TABBY   He was on magazines too, and TV for months.

RICK   I'll stay here and see who's around.

TABBY   You're sure?

RICK   I'll stay here, I think.

TABBY   I really have to say hi to Donna.

RICK   Okay. I'll be here.

TABBY   Okay.

[TABBY *goes.* RICK *talks to* NANCY.]

RICK It was a real battle all right, it cost me this eye. But we hung in there and we did it, and when I got to the treasure there were rubies and there were sapphires packed in there so tight. And there were diamonds, and now we're a major force on the sea. We're smaller than some. We're a small major force. So we're not so widely recognized. But we're expanding. [*To off.*] Connie Cummings. Connie.

[CONNIE *enters. She's Santa Claus.*]

CONNIE [*To* RICK.] Stuart Beamish? Oh, hi.

RICK Rick Arzoomanian. Remember?

CONNIE Rick, so you're a pirate, and Nancy you're a giraffe, what great things to be.

RICK I'm a pirate all right, Connie.

CONNIE It's a terrific time to be a pirate. And to be a giraffe.

RICK And you're Santa Claus.

CONNIE It's strange sometimes, to actually be the real Santa.

RICK Sure.

CONNIE To really be based in the North Pole. To actually fly the whole globe in one night.

RICK It must be something.

CONNIE Everybody makes a big deal about how I'm the first woman Santa and that's great, what it says to girls and what it means.

RICK Sure.

CONNIE   But on a day-to-day basis it's much more about dealing with the media. Protecting the image, making it fresh for a new millennium.

RICK   Sure.

CONNIE   The elves handle construction pretty much on their own but you have to keep an eye on that, and deal with reindeer unions.

RICK   Uh-huh.

CONNIE   But when winter rolls around it's still about the joy, bringing joy to the world.

RICK   I'd been getting nowhere on land, year after year.

CONNIE   Uh-huh.

RICK   So I got a crew together and headed to sea and I saw this ship, and I had a feeling, that it was ready for new ownership and so we took it on and—

CONNIE   Uh-huh.

RICK   And when I opened the treasure I saw, there was—

[BRANDON *enters. He's a warlock.*]

BRANDON   Connie Cummings. Brandon Tavelle. Remember?

CONNIE   So you're a witch.

BRANDON   [*Wounded.*] I'm not a witch, I'm a warlock.

CONNIE   What a great thing to be, Brandon.

BRANDON   Always knew I had something. Through all the crap I endured. The winking and whispering at those cliquey drinking parties. Anthony Oaks and Sally Bottini. Or Little Miss Muppet and her brainless cronies in the back of the lecture hall saving four seats with an apple so they could point at me and giggle. Or the marching-band-lacrosse-gang with their esoteric handshakes and midnight sing-songs, which they always topped off with the obligatory run down the hallway to howl their lewd nicknames and puke in my shoes. I wanted to jump off the tower, but I buried myself in the library, found this book about spells and my God that was me. I could pull toads out of people's ears. I could turn those toads into snakes, and make the snakes disappear in a burst of flame. I knew I could do it, and now: I do. And it has this effect. A power. Not just on my parents. Total strangers come up to me, with this look, you can see it. They open their mouths, not a damn sound comes out, because they're speechless.

CONNIE   It's a terrific time to be in witchcraft.

BRANDON   [*Destroyed.*] I'm not a witch. I'm a warlock.

[BRANDON *storms off.*]

RICK   And when I opened the treasure there were rubies. And sapphires. And diamonds. And they were all packed in there so tight.

CONNIE   Huh.

RICK   Emeralds and rubies, and silver, there was silver in there. And I felt shocked and I felt proud, and so lucky, that it was all right there, all at once. Everything I needed was right at my feet, we'd gone from struggling to stay afloat to being a major force. And now the heat doesn't bother us, and the wind is no problem. We're going in just the right direction as a major force on the sea.

CONNIE   When I go flying on Christmas Eve I go down the chimney of everybody, every person on earth, rich and poor, every nation, from home to home to home it's such a rush as you get going, you get into this rhythm and it's intoxicating.

RICK   It must be.

CONNIE   To make their lives so full and so special with these things they've been dying for all year, things they want and they need that are thrilling and wholesome, pure joy that's really good for them, electric and lasting and real.

RICK   That's something.

CONNIE   To drop off their dreams and head back to the sky and hear billions of people gasping and screaming your name, can you imagine?, giving intensely personal perfect pleasure to every human being on earth and having that be your job?, it's not even a job, it's a privilege, I'm tremendously fortunate to be able to make life on earth worth living and bring the entire planet to this state of indescribable ecstasy again and again, there's nothing like it.

RICK   Huh.

CONNIE   And the next day and the next, to see entire families still caught in the glow of this golden moment and know you've lifted their hearts and brought a sense of hope and dignity and given them the strength to grow and really reach for their dreams and to feel in your gut that every chimney you went down was completely worthwhile.

RICK   M.

CONNIE   The stockings hung with glee for God's sake, and the cookies and milk by the fireplace, and the songs all over the radio and TV specials on every network with every major pop star they can drag out singing your praise and the drawings, entire kindergarten classes doing drawings and collages and plays, and your picture's on their lunch boxes, I mean, couldn't you die?

[RICK *nods.*]

There's nothing else I could stand for three seconds after this, any other work would be torture because absolutely nothing else gives such undisputed pleasure with total universal recognition and I'm so ridiculously lucky to be doing exactly what I'm doing, I could laugh every second of my blessed and spectacular life. [*To off.*] Hey, Stuart Beamish. It's me. Connie Cummings. I'm fucking Santa Claus.

[CONNIE *goes.* RICK *gasps for breath, staggers, fists clenched, suffocating.*]

RICK   She's lucky, all right. Her uncle was Santa Claus. Like that didn't help. If my uncle was Santa Claus, I'd be handing out presents. But my uncle wasn't Santa Claus. I was on my own. Knocking on doors. Dying in the heat. Till I saw that ship. And there was rubies. And silver. And diamonds. Where's Chris Dumars?

[RICK *staggers away, falls, crawls off. NANCY stands there. TABBY runs on, laughing and sobbing hysterically.*]

TABBY   Oh, Nancy, hi, did you know Donna Cunningham is pregnant, it's so great, they'd been trying for so long, and she's got this great guy, he gets along great with her friends, and Rich Kravitz has these adorable girls and the sweetest wife, and Sarah Burk's about to have her fourth, and Bob is such a great dad, and I'm finally working on manuscripts that really mean something to me, they're new and beautiful and fresh and so strong, I can go out and push with every muscle in my body, every cell, all my blood and my skin and my guts and my soul.

[TABBY *runs off. NANCY stands there. ALAN enters, stepping carefully, struggling for balance.*]

ALAN   Nancy McCann! I'm Alan Roads! I was in your freshman comp! You wrote such great papers! I used to follow you across the green! Gary Fine and Gary Bowman said I should stop stalking you and ask you out! Meanwhile I didn't know Gary and Gary were going out with each other! I sure wish they were here now but they're dead! All my friends are gone and I have nothing to say and no idea what I'm doing! Hey, the music's starting, let's dance, Nancy McCann! You had great ideas and now your head's way up in the trees and I'm still down here, but I'd feel way up there if you'd dance with me! So let's dance, Nancy McCann! Can we dance?

NANCY   Yes.

[*A pop tune from years ago plays, such as "We Are Family." ALAN holds on to NANCY. ALAN and NANCY begin to dance. RICK and TABBY enter dancing together.*]

[*At first the dancing is self-conscious.* ALAN *and* NANCY *are timid and reserved.* RICK *and* TABBY *dance cautiously, carefully showing off to one another. But as they continue to dance, both couples let go, become more expressive, joyous, and free.* CONNIE *joins the dancing, as do* BRANDON *and* SARAH.]

• • •

Captain
Abalone

Adam Kraar

Adam Kraar

Adam Kraar's plays include *New World Rhapsody* (commissioned by Manhattan Theatre Club, produced at H.B. Playwrights Foundation); *The Spirit House* (premiered at Performance Network of Ann Arbor); *The Abandoned El* (premiered at Illinois Theatre Center); *The Lost Cities of Asher* (New River Dramatists Fellowship); and *Freedom High* (winner of the Handel Playwright Fellowship from the Woodstock Byrdcliffe Arts Guild).

Kraar was a playwriting fellow in residence at Manhattan Theatre Club. His plays have been produced and developed in New York by Ensemble Studio Theatre, Primary Stages, New York Stage and Film, New York Shakespeare Festival, Cherry Lane Theatre, The Lark, Abingdon, Urban Stages, Queens Theatre in the Park, and Theatreworks U.S.A.; and regionally at Geva Theatre, Alliance Repertory Company, New Jersey Rep, New York State Theatre Institute, Bloomington Playwrights Project, Key West Theatre Festival, and others.

Awards: Sewanee Writers' Conference, Bloomington Playwrights Project, Virtual Theatre Project, and the Southeastern Theatre Conference. Fellowships: William Inge Center for the Arts and the Millay Colony. Plays published by: Dramatic Publishing, Smith & Kraus, Sundance Publishers, and Applause Books. Adam grew up in India, Thailand, Singapore, and the U.S., earned an M.F.A. from Columbia University, and lives in Brooklyn with his wife, Karen.

Captain Abalone premiered at the H.B. Playwrights Theatre in June 2002. It was directed by Susan Einhorn, with original music by Skip LaPlante. The cast was as follows:

MARIE, Katherine Hiler

ABE, Matthew Hoverman

persons

MARIE, a youngish woman, who also plays NURSE, an older woman

ABE, a youngish man, who also plays an elderly version of himself

place

The beach

time

The present, and the past, where all young lovers are always young

• • •

[*The beach. A wooden walkway leads down to the water. Enter* NURSE, *seemingly old, wearing nurse's uniform and sunglasses, pushing a wheelchair with* ABE *in it.* ABE, *seemingly elderly, is in a faded bathrobe.*]

NURSE   Old man, old man, what do you want from my life? Such a fuss! There's no need for your grumbly monster conniptions.

ABE   I'm not an old man!

[*The* NURSE *does not hear him.*]

NURSE   We're here! The beach! . . . What is it?

ABE I'm not an old man! I'm 29!

NURSE [*Not hearing him.*] You had your oatmeal and raisins. Look, look how blue it is today.

ABE [*Frustrated.*] AAAAH!!

NURSE Is that what's bugging you? The perfect blue of a perfect day? . . . Like a promise that was never kept.

ABE Yes!

NURSE I fell in love on this beach, before the boardwalk, or the condos, or the condoms. Came here with my heart in a bottle, intending to toss it into the deep—but then I saw him. Leaping off a dune, shining, soaring, flying into the sky and then landing in the sand on two feet, like a god.

[*Beat.*]

I hope you don't mind my telling you. Old man, are you all right?

ABE I'm 14! In my pants, in my chest—

NURSE [*Reminiscing again.*] He became captain of my heart, designer of my destiny— [*To* ABE.] Your nose. You need the stuff.

ABE Oh, no. No. NO!

[NURSE *takes out a jar of sunblock and applies it to* ABE'*s nose.*]

NURSE I did this for my captain. He liked it. Every pore of his perfect body I took care of, better than my own. He would thank me, sometimes, if I urged out a blackhead. He didn't know—he never knew—I loved taking care of him.

[*Affectionately scolding.*]

Hold still, old man.

ABE   I'm 22! Invincible! You'll see!

NURSE   [*Finished putting on sunblock.*] Was that so bad?

[NURSE *turns to look at the ocean. She takes off her sunglasses. Remembering.*]

Captain...

ABE   Old man. Old man. No! I'm...29.

[*With that,* ABE *stands up and throws off his robe, becoming a fit young man wearing nothing but bathing trunks.* NURSE *seems not to notice.*]

Listen! You hear that?! The surf on the sand in Bali, in Ceylon, in Rio, in Paradise. All the sounds from inside all the shells come from this beach, this day!

[*Music: A soaring, somewhat martial air, played by a merry-go-round organ.* ABE *does cartwheels and backflips on the beach.*]

Look at this! Alley, alley... ka-zam!—You're not looking!

NURSE   [*Somewhat absently.*] You know I can't really see.

ABE   You can hear the wind whipping 'round my flipping shins. Listen: Alley alley koop... Ka-zam! Did you hear that?

NURSE   [*Suddenly.*] Yes!

ABE   [*Affectionately.*] Liar!

[NURSE *tosses away her nurse's uniform and stands revealed as* MARIE, *a young woman in a bathing suit.*]

MARIE   Ka-zam!

ABE   Magoo! My luscious Magoo!

[*The music stops.* ABE *addresses the audience.*]

> For you see, my sweet Marie could not see without her
> glasses. On the roller coaster they'd flown off her perfect
> nose, and a god reached out from a cloud and grabbed
> them. I swear! We scoured the ground for an hour, no
> glasses. Then a thunderhead gathered overhead, and
> standing on top of it, wearing her glasses, an angry...
> old...man.
>
> [*Beat.*]
>
> Ohhhh, she is beautiful. She can't see me, but she is full of
> me. And all I see are a million pairs of deep, slightly
> unfocused, tadpole-brown eyes.

[*Music resumes.*]

> And now, never before attempted on Paradise Beach, the
> triple-ripple flip and flex! I will need my assistant for this
> one. Come!

MARIE   ...Okay.

[ABE *ceremoniously leads* MARIE *downstage, then lies on the beach on his back.*]

ABE   [*To audience.*] I must ask for total silence.

> [*Summoning her.*]
>
> Marie.

[MARIE *climbs on top of* ABE; *he puts his feet on her sides and supports her hands with his hands. (Note: The exact acrobatics of this are not important, as long as it evokes two young lovers playing on the beach.) Music flourishes as* ABE *lets go of one of* MARIE's *hands.*]

Her head is above the clouds! What do you see, Marie?

MARIE   You know I can't see.

ABE   Feel around. Are your glasses up there?

MARIE   No! Let me down.

ABE   I would never let you down. You are my firmament, my
foundation, my—

MARIE   Come on. Your nose is burning up.

[ABE *lets her down.* MARIE *pantomimes taking out a jar of sunblock and applying it to his nose. The music has stopped.*]

ABE   . . . Thank you.

MARIE   I like doing it. You have a perfect nose.

ABE   So do you.

MARIE   Mine has blemishes, and a bump.

ABE   I could eat that bump, and never again be hungry.

MARIE   You want lunch? I picked you up a seafood salad.

ABE   Oh, darling! How did you know?

[MARIE *walks upstage to the cabana to get the lunch;* ABE *watches her.*]

[*To the audience.*]

Look at those calves—*baby!* Those little feet—dainty, pliant, *delicious!* That contentment! She knows, she knows, she belongs on this beach with me; always has, always will. There is no other beach, no other world, no old man in the clouds—

[*To himself.*]

. . . Or is there?

[MARIE *returns with a (pantomimed) plastic container and a towel. She lays out the "towel" and sets up the lunch for* ABE, *who sits on the towel.*]

MARIE   How does it look?

ABE   A feast!

MARIE   It's got scallops, shrimp, oysters, tuna and fresh abalone.

ABE   Abalone! Remember the abalone we had in Babylon?

[MARIE *blushes.*]

MARIE   Eat.

[ABE *eats.*]

[*To audience.*]

I love to watch him eat. He loves food more than he loves my body, and that's healthy. My body won't always be this perfect, but I can always give him fresh abalone.

[ABE *picks around in the salad.*]

[*To* ABE.]

What is it? Is something off?

ABE   Well...

MARIE   If anything looks doubtful, don't eat it. Remember the sushi we had in Chattahoochee?

ABE   I asked you never to mention that!

MARIE   I'm just saying...You have to be careful.

ABE   The shrimp...

MARIE   What, what?

ABE   It's...bad.

MARIE   Oh my God. What does it look like?

ABE   It's brown.

MARIE   EWWWW!

ABE   And there seem to be...

MARIE   What?

ABE   Tiny...creatures—

MARIE   I'm so sorry!

ABE   I can eat around it.

MARIE   No! Throw it away!

ABE   It's fine.

MARIE   You're hungry! And I ate the last banana!

ABE   It's okay.

MARIE   I wasn't hungry. I didn't need that banana. But I figured, he has a whole seafood salad. I thought you'd like it.

ABE   I do! I do!

MARIE   I'm sorry! You're stuck with a blind, stupid—

ABE   No! *Look!* Tiny creature, happy in its yummy home.

MARIE   You cannot eat that salad.

ABE   [*Looking at salad.*] Something's happening.

MARIE   Just throw it away.

ABE   Shhh! It's spinning...pulsating...changing!

MARIE   Really?

ABE   A little red dot. Orange. Oh my god! Growing!

MARIE   Truly?

ABE   Look! It's glowing!

MARIE   I, I can't—

ABE   It's turning into something wonderful.

[ABE *reaches into the container.*]

MARIE   Should you?

ABE   It needs...the ocean.

[ABE *has something on the tip of his finger. He walks downstage towards the ocean.*]

Oh God.

MARIE What?!

ABE A rainbow fish! A flying, fourteen-color manta ray! Can't you see it at all?

[MARIE *doesn't answer. Perhaps, upstage, colors are seen.*]

Ahhh!...It's in the ocean. I can see it, flying through the water.

MARIE Wow!

[*Turning to the audience.*]

I couldn't see the manta ray, but I could see him, basking, proud, tall.

ABE [*To the audience.*] You should've seen her! Proud, her cheeks glowing with blood and milk and sparkling salt!...And I couldn't, I didn't want her to see...Fool!—To tell her. [*In a passionate reverie, towards her, though she doesn't hear him.*] This day forever! You, me; you, you, you! I love you; I love you more than this life!

[MARIE *turns to him.*]

MARIE What happened to your finger?

ABE My finger. Part of the fish got stuck to my finger.

MARIE I hope it's not...

ABE   I can't get it off... but I don't care.

MARIE   Maybe you should. Remember that tar in Myanmar?

ABE   I'm keeping it.

MARIE   Well... You're not touching me with that hand.

ABE   [*Playfully.*] Oh yes, I am.

MARIE   Oh no, you're not. You know I'm susceptible.

ABE   [*Chasing her.*] Fish man! His tentacles are orange! His soul is ink!

MARIE   [*Playfully.*] Stay away!

ABE   Heh-heh-heh-heh...

[ABE *pursues* MARIE. *She runs, and abruptly vanishes.*]

Darling? Darling?

[*Pause. To audience.*]

Something had been growing in her all along. I saw it but I didn't know it. And suddenly... she was gone.

[*For four seconds, we hear the sound of the ocean.*]

[*To audience.*]

You see it? Skidding through the green aquamarine, magenta wings unfurling, pushing as it rises, then bursts out of the white crest and she soars into the sky, in an arc that etches itself across your heart forever.

[*Pause.* NURSE *enters upstage, again wearing uniform and glasses. She stands near the empty wheelchair.*]

NURSE   [*Addressing "ABE" in the empty wheelchair.*] Could you believe I was once hot? "Hot Mamma" he called me, once in a while; never called me my name. I never wanted a name except his name.

[*Pause.*]

I'm not sorry. After all, now I have you. I wonder what's gotten into us today. Old man, are you all right? Are you in there?

[ABE *is downstage, facing audience.*]

ABE   Darling? Watch this: Here I come!

[*For a moment,* ABE *raises his arms in a heroic flourish, on the verge of taking a great leap. Sound of crashing waves swell as the lights fade to black.*]

• • •

The Changing of the Guard

Amy Staats

Amy Staats

Amy Staats lives in Williamsburg, Brooklyn, with her husband, Jeff, and her cat, Flip. Through her involvement as an actress in the creation of new plays, she has been inspired to write herself. Her first full-length play, *Move*, was the recipient of a New Voices fellowship and received readings at the New Group and the Ensemble Studio Theatre. *The Changing of the Guard*, her first one-act play, was produced in the Ensemble Studio Theatre's Marathon 2003 alongside John Guare and Tina Howe. She has just finished a new full-length, entitled *Good Times/Bad Times*, which was workshopped in 2006 at E.S.T's Lexington Retreat. Works in progress include a screenplay, entitled *Mr. Rawls*, and *Cat.her.in.e*, which she will be performing as a solo piece.

This play is for Goggie, who taught me so much and who I miss every day even though I know she's around.

The Changing of the Guard was originally performed at the Ensemble Studio Theatre's Marathon 2003; directed by Mark Roberts.

The cast was as follows:

> **MAMA SUE**   Scotty Bloch
>
> **ELEANOR**   Diana Ruppe
>
> **CONSTANCE**   Julie Leedes

characters

> **CONSTANCE**, 22-ish, first-year graduate student majoring in business. She is still living in her hometown of Baltimore, MD
>
> **ELEANOR**, 20-ish, her younger sister. She is a dancer and has been living in New York City for two years
>
> **MAMA SUE**, late 70s. An old-school Baltimore society lady in the best sense of the word

• • •

[*Present time. Very nice hotel room in London, England.* ELEANOR, *20, and* CONSTANCE, *22, are asleep in their beds. There is a knock at the door.*]

MAMA SUE   [*From behind door.*] Constance! Eleanor! Girrrrls! Are you up?

ELEANOR and CONSTANCE   Mmmmmmph.

MAMA SUE   Are you up?

[MAMA SUE *fumbles behind the door with her card key.*]

ELEANOR [*To* CONSTANCE.] What time is it?

CONSTANCE 7:34.

ELEANOR Fuck.

[ELEANOR *takes the comforter and wraps herself up in a ball.*]

CONSTANCE Good morning, Mama Sue, we're up.

ELEANOR [*To* CONSTANCE.] Kiss ass.

MAMA SUE [*Still behind door.*] Very good, darling. Is Eleanor up?

ELEANOR [*Still asleep.*] I'm up, I'm up. Connie, tell her I'm up.

MAMA SUE Be sure and make her get up. Tell her not to dawdle. Your grandfather and I were up every morning at 6:30 on the nose.

ELEANOR On the nose. [*Overlap.*] Jesus.

CONSTANCE Shhhhh. She's up, Mama Sue.

MAMA SUE What?

ELEANOR I'm up.

MAMA SUE Very well, then. Constance, tell Eleanor if she's going to do her dance exercises, she'd better get up and do them now.

ELEANOR Holy mother of God, my head is gonna fucking explode.

CONSTANCE [*To* ELEANOR.] Shhhhh.

MAMA SUE   Tell her we have to be sure to get to Buckingham Palace nice and early so we have a view. We want to be sure and see their hats. It's no fun if we can't see their hats. And the key. We want to be sure and see them pass the key. Tell Eleanor if we get there late, there won't be any point. We won't be able to see anything at all.

ELEANOR   [*Under breath.*] It's frickin' 7:30. The ceremony starts at eleven. At eleven.

CONSTANCE   Okay, Mama Sue.

MAMA SUE   And please remind her that we leave for Scotland this evening, so our bags need to be packed and ready to go. We have to be at the Royal Mews by 1:00 if we want to see the gold carriage before lunch.

ELEANOR   Jesus fucking mother of God.

CONSTANCE   Shh . . .

MAMA SUE   What did you say?

CONSTANCE   Shh. Nothing. Ellie just sneezed.

MAMA SUE   Oh dear. Tell her not to get sick. She cannot get sick.

ELEANOR   Oh my God.

CONSTANCE   Ellie's not sick. She just sneezed.

MAMA SUE   That's what you get for trouping around in the middle of the night to go to some pub till goodness knows what hour. Now if Eleanor's sick . . .

CONSTANCE Ellie's not sick and we only had one beer.

ELEANOR [*To* CONSTANCE.] Liar.

MAMA SUE Very well. Tell Eleanor she absolutely cannot get sick. And make sure she's up and tell her to brush her hair.

CONSTANCE Okay, Mama Sue.

MAMA SUE Very well, girls. I'm going to put on my face. Knock on my door when you're ready to go down to breakfast.

CONSTANCE Yes, ma'am, I will.

MAMA SUE Very good.

[MAMA SUE *exits to her room.*]

ELEANOR Jesus Christ. I'm not gonna brush it. I'm gonna rat it up extra freaky.

[*Pause.*]

I haven't ratted my hair since the cock-sucking eighth grade.

CONSTANCE Ellie, don't be a spaz. If we're going ahead with the plan, we need to handle it in the most gently democratic way possible. Do you understand what I'm saying?

ELEANOR Sure. Absolutely.

CONSTANCE I mean, she is paying for everything. That does give her a certain inalienable right to tell us what to do.

ELEANOR   Right.

CONSTANCE   We must remember that we're really very lucky.

ELEANOR   Right.

CONSTANCE   Very, very lucky.

[*Pause.*]

ELEANOR   I can't believe we have to get up at the break of dawn and see the stupid fucking cock-sucking guards exchange a stupid fucking key. It starts at 11:00. Why the fuck do we have to get up at 7:30? Huh? Why?

[*Pause. Silence.*]

CONSTANCE   When you use language like that it makes me feel really sad.

[*Pause.*]

ELEANOR   Sad? Sad, like how?

CONSTANCE   It's creepy, Eleanor. When you use that word you sound like you're trying to be tough.

[*Pause.*]

ELEANOR   Which word sounds creepy, fuck or cock?

   [*Silence.*]

   Cock, right?

[*Pause.*]

CONSTANCE   I just think we need to examine our tactics. If
Mama Sue heard you talking like that, she'd be really hurt.

ELEANOR   I sound like I'm trying to be tough?

CONSTANCE   Yes. Well, sometimes.

ELEANOR   Well, why didn't you say something before? I must
have said cock a million times in the last week. Why are
you suddenly telling me now?

CONSTANCE   Because I just realized at this moment that I had a
problem with it. Don't worry, it's not a big deal.

ELEANOR   Okay.

CONSTANCE   It made me feel uncomfortable, but I didn't want
to embarrass you.

ELEANOR   I'm not trying to be tough. This is who I am. This is
me.

CONSTANCE   Well, I certainly don't want to discourage you
from expressing yourself.

[*Pause.*]

ELEANOR   Right.

CONSTANCE   The first thing we need to do is to gently
introduce the idea of a slight variation in the itinerary.

ELEANOR   Right.

CONSTANCE   We'll say: Look, don't get us wrong, we are
having a wonderful time and we completely appreciate
your generosity...

ELEANOR   Right.

CONSTANCE   And we understand that before Granddaddy died you came to England once a year and this is the schedule you both had enjoyed, but I just finished exams and am completely exhausted and Ellie is performing a solo in three weeks and really needs to do her Pilate exercises and we would love to discuss the possibility of not seeing the Changing of the Guards. The *Rough Guide* said it was overrated, and it's not an aspect of London that particularly interests us now that we're older.

ELEANOR   Right.

CONSTANCE   It's such a simple thing. We have a common goal here: We all want to have a good time.

[*Pause.*]

ELEANOR   You don't think Mama Sue heard me, do you?

CONSTANCE   Heard you do what?

ELEANOR   Swear.

CONSTANCE   I don't know.

   [*Pause.*]

   Maybe she did.

[*Pause.*]

ELEANOR   Oh my God, what if she heard me.

CONSTANCE   Don't freak out, Ellie. What's done is done.

ELEANOR   Shit. I feel really bad. And stupid. I didn't mean it.

CONSTANCE   Don't feel bad. What you're doing now is venting.

ELEANOR   Yes. Right now it's okay to say these things because we are venting.

CONSTANCE   Well, it seems more as if you were venting. I'm not really venting, I'm explaining.

ELEANOR   God.

CONSTANCE   What?

ELEANOR   Nothing.

CONSTANCE   Mmmmm. These sheets are so nice.

ELEANOR   Why can't we for one day go someplace cool like Chelsea or Abbey Road or someplace interesting and vital and, you know, look at people and just hang?

CONSTANCE   I think it would be a tactical error to mention Abbey Road again.

ELEANOR   I mean, I wouldn't. That's just an example.

CONSTANCE   Right.

ELEANOR   I can't believe she almost ran over that guy.

CONSTANCE   Oh, I know... We can't have her drive.

ELEANOR   Right.

CONSTANCE   I think we need to ask her for the keys.

ELEANOR Right… I can't drive, though. You'll have to drive.

CONSTANCE Jesus, Ellie.

ELEANOR What?

CONSTANCE Nothing. It's nothing. Forget about it.

ELEANOR No, what do you mean? Jesus, Connie, I haven't driven in four years.

CONSTANCE I know.

ELEANOR I just think it's stupid for me to try to drive on the left-hand side when I haven't driven in four years after only having driven for two years before the four years. It's not my fault. I live in New York. I have a problem with depth perception.

CONSTANCE I know, I know, I know.

ELEANOR You don't understand me at all.

CONSTANCE Mmm.

[*Falling back asleep.*]

ELEANOR Mama Sue just seems so weird and tense. It's like, she's still trying to treat us like children and we're completely adults now. I've never seen her like this.

CONSTANCE Well, this is what she's like sometimes.

ELEANOR I never noticed.

CONSTANCE Well, you haven't been around.

ELEANOR   Oh, fuck you. Don't you start.

[*Pause.*]

CONSTANCE   I think we need to work on re-establishing our
relationships as adults.

[*Pause.*]

ELEANOR   I think that might be a good idea.

[*Falling back asleep.*]

[*Pause.*]

CONSTANCE   It's really amazing how if you use the right
vocabulary, you can really pinpoint problems and get
people to work together.

[*Pause.*]

ELEANOR   Oh, Connie, I think I'm really hung over. I don't
think I can get up. Are you hungover?

CONSTANCE   [*Hungover.*] Mmmmmm. I'm not sure. I may have
a bit of a headache.

[*Pause.*]

You should drink more water when you drink. Very
important.

ELEANOR   Right.

[*Pause.* CONSTANCE *and* ELEANOR *do not get up.*]

Well, I guess we should get up.

CONSTANCE   Aren't we up already?

ELEANOR   I don't think so.

CONSTANCE   I think we might be up already.

ELEANOR   I'm pretty sure we are.

[*They nod off. MAMA SUE knocks on door.*]

MAMA SUE   Girls?

> [*She knocks again.*]
>
> Girls?
>
> [*Pause.*]
>
> Girls! I have been patiently waiting for you in my room for exactly one half of an hour. One half of an hour.

[CONSTANCE *pops up.*]

CONSTANCE   Shoot.

> [CONSTANCE *shakes* ELEANOR.]
>
> Ellie, wake up.
>
> [ELEANOR *wakes up.*]

ELEANOR   Fuck cock.

[ELEANOR *hops out of bed, puts on her headphones, and starts doing vigorous Pilate exercises half-asleep.*]

MAMA SUE   Are you there? Girls? It's 8:04 in the morning!

[MAMA SUE *opens door and peeks her head in.*]

Good heavens! Are you just getting up?

[MAMA SUE *enters. She is a well-dressed woman in her very late seventies. Her outfit is very tasteful and attractive except for her running shoes.*]

CONSTANCE   I'm sorry, Mama Sue. I'm up. We're up.

MAMA SUE   Sleeping till 8:04 in the morning on your last day in London! I can't stand it. I just can't stand it.

CONSTANCE   Look at me. I'm up. We're up.

MAMA SUE   Now we won't have time to have a proper breakfast. We won't have time to do anything at all.

CONSTANCE   Actually, the service doesn't start till eleven.

MAMA SUE   The service starts at 10:30. What is she doing?

CONSTANCE   Her exercises.

MAMA SUE   Oh, for heaven's sakes, there isn't time.

[MAMA SUE *lifts up* ELEANOR'*s headphones.*]

Eleanor!

[ELEANOR *is startled and screams.*]

Oh, for heaven's sakes, stop screaming.

ELEANOR   I didn't mean to.

CONSTANCE   Mama Sue, Ellie didn't mean to scream.

MAMA SUE   Eleanor, we haven't time to do exercises. Get up and get dressed this instant.

ELEANOR What?

MAMA SUE I said get up and get dressed.

ELEANOR I am not a child. Please do not treat me like one.

CONSTANCE Ellie, no.

ELEANOR What?

CONSTANCE Just...relax.

ELEANOR No. She treats me like a child. I am not a child.

CONSTANCE Umm...Mama Sue, I was reading the *Rough Guide* and it says the Changing of the Guards doesn't start until eleven. If we leave at 10:30, we'll have plenty of time for a leisurely breakfast.

MAMA SUE Excuse me?

CONSTANCE It will give us a chance to relax and connect in with each other.

MAMA SUE *Rough Guide, Rough Guide, Rough Guide,* what is it with this *Rough Guide*? If you prefer to trudge about all day with a backpack and hiking boots and eat beans from a can...

CONSTANCE I really like the *Rough Guide*. It really helped me a lot in Tibet. The layout is so specific and clear.

MAMA SUE If that is the kind of trip to England you prefer, you can take a bus to whichever hostile youth center you prefer, but I have been coming to London since before you were born and know for a fact the Changing of the Guards starts at 10:30 and I for one am getting there at 10...

ELEANOR   Maybe call the front desk and find out for sure. It always seems like we get places too early.

MAMA SUE   Excuse me?

CONSTANCE   Ellie, shh.

MAMA SUE   Fine. If you want to call downstairs so we can lounge around at the hotel, if that's what you'd like to do with your time in London, that's fine, but I am getting in the car at 9:30 and driving to Buckingham Palace either by myself or with either or both of my granddaughters.

ELEANOR   Connie and I don't think you should dr—

CONSTANCE   Ellie, no.

[CONSTANCE *gives* ELEANOR *the stare.*]

Mama Sue, I am certainly not trying to argue with you. I'm just suggesting . . .

MAMA SUE   We are not arguing. We are having a discussion. Now I am going down to breakfast and I expect you to be down with your bags packed in twenty minutes, and, Eleanor, I cannot promise to save you a scone.

ELEANOR   I never asked you to save me a scone.

MAMA SUE   What are you talking about? You always ask me to save you a scone.

CONSTANCE   Eleanor doesn't eat scones.

MAMA SUE   Don't you think I would know weather or not my own granddaughter asked me to save her a scone? Of course you asked me, this morning.

ELEANOR   No, I really didn't.

CONSTANCE   Ellie...

MAMA SUE   Sue. Don't be ridiculous! Of course you did. What is the point of telling me you didn't ask me to save you a scone when I remember full well that you did. I can't stand it. I just can't stand it. I am going downstairs. Good morning.

[MAMA SUE *exits.*]

ELEANOR   Jesus. I never asked her to save me a scone. What's wrong with her? She's completely out of control.

[CONSTANCE *starts getting dressed and packing bags.* ELEANOR *gets on the ground and starts her Pilate abdominal exercises.*]

CONSTANCE   Ellie, what are you doing?

ELEANOR   I just have to do my abs, I'll be done in five minutes.

CONSTANCE   Ellie.

ELEANOR   What? I have to get in a white unitard in three weeks, okay? You have no idea what kind of pressure I'm under.

CONSTANCE   Fine.

[CONSTANCE *continues to pack.*]

Don't expect me pack your stuff for you, because I'm not going to do it.

ELEANOR   Fine.

CONSTANCE   Ellie!

ELEANOR   What?

[ELEANOR *advances to the second set of more vigorous Pilates abdominal exercises.* CONSTANCE *stares at her.*]

CONSTANCE   Can't you see that we're in a hurry?

ELEANOR   What are we in a hurry for?

CONSTANCE   Ellie, we have to be downstairs in twenty
minutes!

ELEANOR   I know that.

CONSTANCE   Well, come on, get ready.

ELEANOR   I will.

CONSTANCE   This is not the time to be exercising.

[ELEANOR *turns onto her stomach and starts kicking her arms and legs in the air at the same time like she's swimming.*]

ELEANOR   Why are you so worried about me? Why don't you
get ready, then?

CONSTANCE   Jesus.

ELEANOR   What?

CONSTANCE   Because I know what's gonna happen here. You're
going to be totally late and I'm gonna have to pack up for
you.

ELEANOR   No, you won't, Connie, I'll be fine.

CONSTANCE   Fine.

[ELEANOR *on her side and starts doing a super-fast full Pilates side-kick series.*]

I'm packing up my toothpaste kit. If you want to use my toothpaste, you'd better do it now.

ELEANOR   Okay. Just give me a minute.

CONSTANCE   I'm packing it now, Ellie.

ELEANOR   Fine. Just pack it.

CONSTANCE   You're not gonna brush your teeth?

ELEANOR   I'm gonna brush my teeth.

CONSTANCE   Your not gonna use toothpaste?

ELEANOR   What are you, my mom?

CONSTANCE   No, I'm not. Jesus, you are so inconsiderate.

ELEANOR   What are you talking about?

CONSTANCE   Mama Sue is obviously stressed out, why can't you just do what she wants?

ELEANOR   I know she's stressed out. I am aware of that, okay? But just because I'm not getting ready how you wanna get ready doesn't mean I'm not getting ready.

CONSTANCE   Fine.

[ELEANOR *gets up and casually starts getting dressed.*]

ELEANOR   Can I wear your blue sweater?

CONSTANCE   No.

ELEANOR   Fine. I don't really care.

CONSTANCE   Okay, we've got ten minutes.

ELEANOR   I know, okay, I know. I've got a watch, all right?

CONSTANCE   Fine. Since when do you wear a watch?

ELEANOR   I've had a watch for like a year now.

CONSTANCE   I thought you didn't like to be restricted by time.

ELEANOR   Stop it.

CONSTANCE   Stop what?

ELEANOR   Stop trying to control me.

CONSTANCE   I'm not trying to control you, I'm just repeating what you said.

ELEANOR   I said that like a million years ago.

CONSTANCE   It wasn't that long ago, Ellie.

ELEANOR   I can take care of myself now, Connie.

CONSTANCE   I never said you couldn't.

ELEANOR   I have been living on my own in New York City for two whole fucking years now, Connie.

CONSTANCE   Oh, and a heck of a lot of good it's done you.

[*Knock on the door.*]

MAMA SUE   Girls?

[ELEANOR *and* CONSTANCE *look around the room. It is a mess and nothing has been packed.*]

CONSTANCE   Coming!

ELEANOR   We're coming! Connie, I'll just stuff it all in, you pack up the sink.

CONSTANCE   Okay. Here, just wear my sweater.

ELEANOR   Cool.

MAMA SUE   Constance, Eleanor?

ELEANOR   Connie's just getting dressed.

CONSTANCE   Fuck you.

ELEANOR   Shhh.

MAMA SUE   Oh, for heaven's sakes, I've seen you naked before.

ELEANOR   We're coming.

MAMA SUE   I don't care if you're dressed.

ELEANOR   But we are, we are, we really are.

MAMA SUE   That's wonderful, dear. Just open the door.

CONSTANCE   Open the door, Ellie.

[ELEANOR *opens the door. MAMA SUE is slightly out of breath, rolls in a room-service cart carrying an English breakfast complete with tea, clotted cream, etc.*]

We're ready!

ELEANOR Good morning!

MAMA SUE I walked all the way downstairs and I thought, Sue, you're just being silly. Who wants to go to breakfast all alone when I can eat with my two lovely granddaughters? So this nice girl downstairs packed me up this lovely breakfast and the porter brought it up for me. Isn't that wonderful? We'll just sit on the beds like a bunch of bohemians. Oh, heavens me, my friends would think I was very mod. Here, we'll just put this on the table...

CONSTANCE Ellie. pull up the table.

MAMA SUE Very good. Oh my. Look at that delicious cream. Not that we'll have time to properly enjoy it. What a waste. A waste.

[*Pause. They eat.*]

CONSTANCE Mama Sue, Eleanor and I have been thinking...

MAMA SUE Oh, good heavens, that nice girl gave us some bacon! Henry would have been so pleased. Your grandfather simply adored Irish bacon. Mmm. Eleanor dear, have some bacon.

ELEANOR No thank you.

CONSTANCE So. We've been thinking...

MAMA SUE Have some bacon, Eleanor.

ELEANOR No thank you. I'm a vegetarian.

MAMA SUE   Really? Well, here, just have a little.

CONSTANCE   She hasn't eaten meat in two years.

ELEANOR   It's not a big deal.

MAMA SUE   Well, I for one think that's ridiculous. All you young people running around not eating meat.

CONSTANCE   I eat meat.

MAMA SUE   Pasta, pasta, pasta, that's all anybody wants to eat these days. Your grandfather just couldn't stand it. "What's the big deal about pasta?" he'd say. It's just flour and water. I don't see why people think it's so healthy. I for one prefer rice.

ELEANOR   Okay.

CONSTANCE   So Eleanor and I have been thinking...

MAMA SUE   No nutritive value whatsoever.

CONSTANCE   Ellie and I were thinking that although you and Granddaddy really enjoyed Buckingham Palace there may be certain aspects of London that may be of greater interest to us. We thought it might be fun if all three of us had a discussion about what we'd like to do with our last day in London, and then we could take a vote on it.

MAMA SUE   A vote?

CONSTANCE   Yes.

[*Pause.*]

MAMA SUE Fine.

CONSTANCE Great.

ELEANOR Cool.

MAMA SUE Sounds perfectly fair. If you want to go to pubs till all hours and spend three hours looking for a wall with graffiti all over it...

ELEANOR What?

CONSTANCE [*To* ELEANOR.] Ellie, no. We weren't even out late, Mama Sue. We had two beers and came home.

ELEANOR Abbey Road is a very famous street. I'm really sorry we got lost. It was something I really wanted to see. I'm sorry we were too late to get into The National Portrait Gallery. I'm sorry.

MAMA SUE Oh, it's fine. I thought it might be something you'd like to see, but never mind.

ELEANOR It's not that I didn't want to see it, it just that... never mind.

[*They eat.*]

MAMA SUE So, Constance, what exactly is it that you wished to vote *on*?

CONSTANCE Well, I for one am very interested in visiting the Whitechapel Art Gallery. It stages some of London's most innovative exhibitions of contemporary art, as well as housing the biennial Whitechapel opening, which gives a chance for local artists to get their work shown to a wider audience.

MAMA SUE   Hmmm. Doesn't that sound interesting.

ELEANOR   And I really want to see the Mary Quant exhibit in Chelsea. I'm really into early sixties fashion.

[*Pause.*]

MAMA SUE   Really.

>[*Beat.*]

>How fascinating.

>[*Beat.*]

>With all the important things to look at and do and see when one is in London, you want to go to an exhibit of secondhand clothes from the sixties? If you want to look at old clothes from the sixties, we can make a trip to the barn sale when we get home.

CONSTANCE   Mama Sue, that's not fair.

ELEANOR   They're not regular clothes. It's couture.

CONSTANCE   It's an aspect of London that really interests her.

MAMA SUE   Really? How fascinating.

>[*Beat.*]

>I can't stand it. I just can't stand it. With all of the wonderful, elegant things one can learn and grow from I cannot understand why you are so attracted to the gutter.

CONSTANCE Mama Sue. She can't help it. She's been living in New York.

MAMA SUE Such a pretty girl. And you shroud yourself in black. Black, black, black.

ELEANOR I'm wearing blue.

MAMA SUE Staying out in pubs all night, going to thrift stores. I can't stand it. I just can't stand it.

ELEANOR I think there's beauty in people. Not just buildings and palaces and *things*. It's just so *limited*.

CONSTANCE Ellie...

MAMA SUE Limited! You call Buckingham Palace and the Houses of Parliament *limited*! You call Westminster Abbey *limited*! All that beautiful stone...

CONSTANCE That's not what she means...

MAMA SUE *Reaching* to the sky...

ELEANOR It *is* what I mean, Connie. It's *exactly* what I mean... Buckingham palace is boring. It's a boring, ugly castle.

CONSTANCE Ellie...

MAMA SUE Boring? You call it boring? Do you know what went on there, during the war? Why do you think the Germans bombed it again and again? It stood for *order*, it stood for *continuity*, it stood for *tradition*.

ELEANOR It's just a *building*. There's nothing interesting happening *inside* it. Just stuffy old people saying old stuffy things.

CONSTANCE   Ellie, no.

MAMA SUE   Stuffy old people...? How dare you! How dare you speak to me that way! Don't you realize... Don't you realize, Eleanor Hopkins, that those old stuffy people were young once too? They had lives ten times richer than you could possibly imagine. Why? Why do young people insist they were the first. You have no idea. No idea at all. Nobody, nobody, nobody, Harry, how could you? How could you leave me without any warning? You weren't even sick. I didn't know... I wasn't prepared. Goddamnit.

[*Pause.*]

CONSTANCE   Right now there's a lot of tension and miscommunication between us. But I'm sure if we pinpoint what's really bugging us, we can easily find a solution.

[*Pause. They eat.*]

MAMA SUE   Listen to me carrying on like a sorry sport...

CONSTANCE   You're not a sorry sport.

MAMA SUE   I suppose I miss him more than I let on. He was a good talker, your grandfather.

[*Pause. They eat.*]

If you think you are the first young lady to disagree with her elders, Ms. Eleanor, you are sadly mistaken. Your mother thought the sixties where radical, but that was nothing, *nothing* compared to the twenties. *Nothing.*

[*Pause. They eat.*]

I guess I wanted to take you to the places Harry and I had loved. I suppose I had an idea in my dumb head of how it would work out.

CONSTANCE   I think it's working out great.

ELEANOR   Yeah. I really am having a wonderful time.

MAMA SUE   Well, I'm glad.

> [*They eat.*]

Before your grandfather died he got very affectionate with me, but it wasn't always like that. He never wanted to travel, he didn't want to do anything fun. One day I said *fine* and I called my friend June and said, "Look, June, let's go to Europe," and off we went. 1968. He was so mad. He thought it wasn't decent. He didn't speak to me afterwards for two weeks... but eventually... he did. One morning at breakfast I found two tickets under my grapefruit. London, first class. We went on the same trip every year for twenty years. It was wonderful. It saved our marriage.

CONSTANCE   I didn't know that you and Granddaddy ever fought.

MAMA SUE   Do you think it was easy? Being married for so long? It wasn't easy, girls. We had to work at it. Bit by bit. Stone by stone. You have to work to build things. And in the end... you have something. You have something nice. Then suddenly... it's gone. Typical.

> [*Pause. They eat.*]

It's all very discouraging. Not being able to wear nice shoes. I used to have the slimmest ankles just like you girls. If I had ankles like that again, I'd walk all day.

[*Pause.*]

I suppose that's the nice thing about a building. It's not like a body... the outside... the outside remains the same, it's the inside that's transitory. Unless there's a bomb or an earthquake or something hideous. What on earth am I talking about? I get to the end of these sentences and have no idea how I got there. It's the funniest thing. Oh, look! They gave us bacon. How wonderful. Your grandfather simply adored Irish bacon. He simply adored it.

[*Pause.*]

ELEANOR   These crumpets are delicious. The way the crispy holes hold the butter.

MAMA SUE   Yes, they are. They certainly are.

[*Pause. They eat.*]

CONSTANCE   What time is it?

ELEANOR   9:27.

CONSTANCE   We should watch the time. If we want to make it to Buckingham Palace by 10:30, we should watch the time.

ELEANOR   What?

[CONSTANCE *nudges* ELEANOR.]

Right.

MAMA SUE   Oh, we don't have to go see the soldiers if you don't want to. If it's not what interests you. We can just stay here, I suppose, for a while and slowly nibble. Have some clotted cream for your scone, Eleanor. Mercy, look at that delicious cream.

CONSTANCE   Mama Sue, we'd like to see the Changing of the Guards.

ELEANOR   Yeah, we really want to go.

MAMA SUE   Oh, pooh. We don't have to go if you really don't want to. We can just sit here and have just a little bit more of this nice marmalade on our toast.

ELEANOR   I just remembered how you talked about them with us when we were little. How they'd march with the tall hats and the red jackets and how straight they stood when the key was exchanged.

MAMA SUE   Did I talk about them?

CONSTANCE   When we were little. You'd tell stories.

MAMA SUE   Did I? I don't remember. Mercy. I do like sitting here. Just sitting here with my two nice granddaughters. I'm so lucky to have such nice grandchildren. We used to have cream like this when we visited the farm in Kentucky when I was small. It would go plop, plop into our cereal bowls. Completely unpasteurized. Nobody worried about cholesterol then.

ELEANOR   Well, we should watch the time, though. If we want to make it to Buckingham Palace by 10:30, we should watch the time.

MAMA SUE   Yes, Eleanor, you're absolutely right. We need to keep track of the time.

[*They continue to eat. They take their time with breakfast and do not get up.*]

Where are you, Mr. Marmalade? On the spoon, there you go.

[*They continue to eat. Nobody gets up.* MAMA SUE *reaches into her handbag, gets out keys, and hands them to* CONSTANCE.]

MAMA SUE   Stupid left-side driving. I never could get used to it.

CONSTANCE   Maybe we can wait till next year to do all the new things. We can wait, and really plan it out, so we know what we're doing.

ELEANOR   That's a good idea. Let's be really traditional today.

CONSTANCE   That sounds like fun. What do you think, Mama Sue?

MAMA SUE   Oh, fine, dear, that's fine. Whatever you want.

ELEANOR   Like, next Thanksgiving, I'll definitely come home. We'll plan it all out together.

CONSTANCE   I really think if we plan it all out, we can be more efficient with our time.

ELEANOR   Definitely, next year. I don't understand why the tea is so good here. It's just so good, it's never like this at home.

MAMA SUE   That's so true. Maybe it's the cream.

ELEANOR   I want to start having tea time in New York. Like, can you imagine? Like, Oh my God, you guys could come up on the train and I could meet you at Penn Station and we could go the Plaza or someplace really grand. Just for the day. Completely extravagant. We could dress up like those ladies in *Eloise*. We could wear ridiculous hats.

CONSTANCE   I'm not wearing a hat.

MAMA SUE   Wouldn't that be something?

• • •

Hermaphrodite

Annie G.

Annie G.

Annie G. is an award-winning and published playwright, screenwriter, and TV writer. In addition to the inclusion of *Hermaphrodite* in *The Best American Short Plays 2002–2003*, she has enjoyed success with other works. Her play *Incommunicado, Inc. or Edge Stew* recently had a performance at Cardboard Box Collaborative in Philadelphia. *Hair of the Dog* has had a few readings in NYC. *It's Only a Test* and *A Well Taught Lesson*, both written for the Brown Ledge Theater in Vermont, are published by Samuel French and are produced throughout the U.S. and the U.K. *G-Force* was seen at the Edinburgh Festival; it, too, is published by Samuel French. *AWOL*, a serial performance art piece ran amuck in nightclubs in L.A. *Something Rotten in Denmark*, winner of a Samuel French award, *Hermaphrodite*, *Open and Shut*, and *What You Want* were performed at the Samuel Beckett Theatre in NYC. *Where's the Party* was produced by ABC-TV.

Annie G. recently finished *Belly of the Beast*, a screenplay, and a brand new play *Deadline*. She studied playwrighting with Bob Moss and Neal Bell.

costume plot

CHRIS 1 and **CHRIS 2**
Matching ties

JEFFREY
Basketball

property plot

Bottle of wine
3 wine glasses
Kitchen towel

sound plot

Timer

cast (in order of appearance)

JEFFREY HUNTER, an archaeologist

CHRIS 1, played by a woman

CHRIS 2, played by a man

• • •

[JEFFREY's *apt.* JEFFREY *is mixing martinis.* CHRIS 1 *and* 2 *are onstage together, their actions are synchronized.*]

JEFFREY   The quiche will be ready in just a few minutes.

CHRIS 1   Smells delicious, Jeffrey. Do real men eat quiche?

JEFFREY   Only when their mothers visit.

CHRIS 1   What ever did you do to this room?

JEFFREY   I renovated. I raised the ceiling by 2 feet, I wanted my basketball hoop regulation height.

CHRIS 1   Interesting.

JEFFREY   [*Hands* CHRIS 1 *a martini.*] Cheers.

[*They raise their glasses.*]

CHRIS 1   How are you, son? It's been much too long, how long has it been?

JEFFREY   Years.

CHRIS 1   Glad you invited me to dinner, saved me a phone call.

JEFFREY   Chairman of a Fortune 500 company, and still counts pennies.

CHRIS 1   Corporate raiders are everywhere, got to be on the plus side of the balance sheet. One sign of weakness and you're done for. Barbarians at the gate, but I've been keeping them at bay. You know me, love the challenge.

JEFFREY   My mother, the toughest businessperson this side of the Tigris Euphrates.

CHRIS 1   Been thinking of you, son.

JEFFREY   Come on, the last time you thought of me was at birth, wondering what the pain was between your legs.

CHRIS 1   You do have a biting tongue.

JEFFREY   I have a couple of other attributes, I keep hoping you'll notice them.

CHRIS 1   I notice a lot more than you realize.

JEFFREY   But always from a distance, my classmates would ask, do you have a mother? And I'd say I'm not sure, I think she's the one who buys me the expensive toys and kisses me good night once a week.

CHRIS 1   What do you want?

JEFFREY   A hug and an apology for having faxed in your motherhood.

CHRIS 1   You didn't ask me here to chastise me about your childhood, did you?

JEFFREY   No. There's an excavation in Someria, an ancient town called Jerada.

CHRIS 1   I should have known.

JEFFREY   Listen for a minute, I think it'll appeal to you. It's believed to be the birthplace of the god Hermaphroditie. Hermaphroditie's one of the few gods to be both male and female. The rediscovery of this god is big-time, we don't know much, only whispers from legends, but her story will have major impact.

CHRIS 1   What are the figures?

[JEFFREY *pulls out a map.*]

JEFFREY   There's a temple dedicated to her buried deep, it's in danger of being destroyed if something isn't done now. If we can excavate, then think of what it could tell us about ourselves.

CHRIS 1   How much more do you want to know about yourself?

JEFFREY   I don't think we ever know enough about ourselves.

CHRIS 1   Haven't I paid for enough of your soul searching?

JEFFREY   A little soul searching would do you some good.

CHRIS 1   Jeffrey, what do I need that for? That's for people who haven't achieved what they wanted.

JEFFREY   Our society is rife with aging businessmen who divorce their wives to marry 20-year-olds. Or rich women who've never dug deep into themselves and feel so shallow that they go and get face-lifts.

CHRIS 1   I never had a face-lift! I need a refill. Haven't I given you enough money?

JEFFREY   [*Grabs the glass and pours the drink.*] Mother, it's not about giving me money. We're talking about a contribution to civilization.

[JEFFREY *hands the martini to* CHRIS 2, *he takes a sip.*]

CHRIS 2   Jeffrey, I love what you did to this room, it's so manly. You have the most clever statues. I suppose you get them from all those interesting third world countries you travel to.

JEFFREY   Yes. I'm surprised but glad you noticed. Mother, this dig is of vital interest to me, and I feel it should be to you too. You always said how hard it was for you to make it in a man's world.

CHRIS 2   Everyone always said Chris Hunter has the body of a woman but the brain of a man.

JEFFREY   Exactly, that's why I feel Hermaphroditie is momentous, she had the full, developed essence of both male and female in a mental, physical, emotional, and spiritual way. Wasn't it you who said, "Only when women start claiming their own divinity can any change towards equality be made on this planet."

CHRIS 2   Did I say that, how clever of me. Are you sure it wasn't one of your other mothers.

JEFFREY   Hermaphroditie was the only goddess to impregnate herself with the full sexual act and gave birth to his own child, a female. This myth calls to a part of me that is awakening, or reawakening.

CHRIS 2   Are you telling me you're pregnant?

JEFFREY   Mother!

CHRIS 1   Well, I don't know, your father was involved in some kinky things.

JEFFREY   You've been divorced from Dad for over 15 years.

CHRIS 2   Your father thinks the more women he beds with the more of a man he is, but the truth is it just makes him more of a dog.

JEFFREY   Come on, Mother, look at me, I'm not my father.

CHRIS 2   Well, look at me, Jeffrey, things haven't been so easy lately. I've been here all this time and you haven't even noticed I had plastic surgery.

JEFFREY   Mother, I don't understand, didn't you just tell me... Sometimes you're like two people...

CHRIS 2   Dr. Whittle. Does everyone. I said to him, give me the works, had my eyes tucked, forehead tucked, chin tucked, breast tucked, tummy tucked and butt tucked. And so, now I look 35. You have no idea what it's like to be a woman.

JEFFREY   I thought you looked fine before, distinguished.

CHRIS 2   Men are distinguished when they get older, but an older woman is considered weak. It's so unfair.

JEFFREY   Mother, you're a battle-ax.

CHRIS 2   That's not a very nice thing to say.

JEFFREY   Well, in a way it is. You're like Lillith, who refused to be subordinate to Adam. So was replaced by Eve. You're a tough cookie. Even though there were times when all I wanted for Christmas was another mother, there were times when I was damned proud.

CHRIS 2   You were proud of me? Really? Oh, Jeffrey, sometimes I don't feel so tough.

JEFFREY   Mom, are you sure it's you speaking?

CHRIS 1   Of course it's me, who else would it be! [*Spills the martini glass.*] Oh, look what I've done.

JEFFREY   No problem, just clean up and refill.

CHRIS 2   Oh, thank you.

[JEFFREY *puts refill on the table in front of them.*]

I've been thinking of you a lot, you don't know how many times I reached for the phone to call you, but something always stopped me.

CHRIS 1   Lost your phone number, son.

CHRIS 2   Your unexpected invitation was so welcome. A prayer out of the blue.

JEFFREY   I didn't know whether to call you or not...

CHRIS 1   Told you last time, the dig at Rayatah would be my last.

JEFFREY   ...but something kept at me. I threw the I-Ching, it was a master hexagram, basically what it said was reach out and touch someone.

CHRIS 2   And here I am! You're quite correct, I am very interested in Hermaphroditie. I do have some questions, though.

CHRIS 1   What are you trying to hit me up for?

JEFFREY   I am requesting a contribution of $300,000.

CHRIS 1   A third of a million to dig in the dessert?

CHRIS 2   I don't see that as a problem.

CHRIS 1   I don't have that kind of money.

JEFFREY   I'm not sure what you're saying. Are you giving me the green light or the red light?

CHRIS 1 and CHRIS 2   Yes.

JEFFREY   I'm confused.

CHRIS 2   Precisely what's happening to me. I don't have the strength I used to.

CHRIS 1   Feeling as strong as ever. My aerobics teacher says I have the stamina of a 30-year-old.

CHRIS 2   Going on 100. You don't know what I've been going through.

JEFFREY   What's going on?

CHRIS 2   They're trying to buy me out.

JEFFREY   Who is?

CHRIS 1   BBB offered a friendly bid, which I immediately rejected but KKP attempted a hostile takeover.

CHRIS 2   I didn't know what to do.

CHRIS 1   KKP played hardball, but I put an immediate clamper on their maladroit attempts to requisition JPD.

CHRIS 2   It took everything out of me.

CHRIS 1   Love the challenge.

CHRIS 2   It started me thinking.

CHRIS 1   Thoughts which I quickly aborted.

CHRIS 2   I've never really lived.

CHRIS 1   I live for the business challenge.

CHRIS 2   But there are more things in life.

CHRIS 1   Work is its own reward.

CHRIS 2   I looked around me and there was no one I could turn to. I've never been close to anyone in my life.

CHRIS 1 Only one you can trust is yourself.

CHRIS 2 And these days I'm not even sure I can do that. Several of my top men were right there pulling for me.

CHRIS 1 With ambitions of their own.

CHRIS 2 I felt so scared.

CHRIS 1 Don't ever let your fears get the best of you, you'll die if you do.

JEFFREY Mother. I've never seen you so fractured.

CHRIS 2 I looked in the mirror the other day, and I had no reflection!

JEFFREY You're exaggerating.

CHRIS 2 I sat down in a chair. I touched my toes, I counted each one. I touched my fingers, I counted each one. I opened a bottle of perfume, yes, I could smell. I put on the radio, I could hear. I rang for lunch, I could eat. I made a phone call. I could talk and I could be heard. I pinched myself, yes, I could feel pain. I went back to the mirror and I still had no reflection!

CHRIS 1 Just a bad day. That's all.

JEFFREY An ancient Mesopotamian belief says that when the shadow disappears, disharmony rules the spirit.

CHRIS 2 I took a bath. And then I thought sell JPD. Sell the goddamn business!

CHRIS 1 Nooooooooo!

[*The next two speeches of* CHRIS 1 *and* 2, *should be simultaneous but interwoven.*]

Achieved everything I've ever wanted, look at my resume.
Took my father's struggling company and made it
something, global, power, I am woman hear me roar. I'm
proud, achievement, build a stronger company, work is
next to godliness. Can't be at every meeting, can't be
everywhere. Be at the helm, in charge, the pilot, feeling the
plane spin out of control, it spins, spinning, spinning. Can't
let go, into the eye of the storm, fly over the storm, can't
let go, hold on tighter, tighter, get control of your
emotions, received an A on my test, Daddy, Chris, you're
too goddamn emotional. One foot in front of another.
Work is its own reward. Keep marching, keep going. If I'm
not at the helm I don't know who I am! Who the hell am I?

CHRIS 2   Life has been one goal, next goal, marry that handsome
man, have a child, chairman of the board, divorce that no
good clout, goal, goal, goal, goal, achieve, achieve, work,
work, work. Build a stronger company, work. Presentation
with important client, walked right out in middle of
speech, walked for hours, days, years, raining, snowing,
hail, where am I going, do I have any money? The room
was spinning, spinning, the earth is spinning, down the
vortex, down the hatchet, down the rabbit hole, drink me,
eat me, through the looking glass, shattered glass, fragile.
Who can I turn to? One foot in front of another.
Earthquake, what is that rumble, fearing my heartbeat.
Where am I, where did I go? Who the hell am I? Who the
hell am I!

JEFFREY   Ma, Ma, Ma, you're not making any sense, you're
barely speaking English.

CHRIS 1 Can't desert the ship.

CHRIS 2 Who the hell am I?

JEFFREY You're obviously in pain.

CHRIS 1 Can't desert the ship.

CHRIS 2 Who the hell am I?

JEFFREY Mom, it's okay, it's okay.

CHRIS 2 40 days, 40 nights, continuous rain.

CHRIS 1 Don't shoot till you see the whites of their eyes.

JEFFREY I'm here for you. I'll figure something out. You can't go on as you have.

CHRIS 1 I've got to, what else do I have?

JEFFREY I'll have to take care of you.

CHRIS 1 Take care of business.

CHRIS 2 Can't take the business.

JEFFREY Ma, when was the last time you took a vacation?

CHRIS 2 I never take vacations.

CHRIS 1 Vacations are for the weak.

JEFFREY You've got to slow down. Come with me to Jerada.

CHRIS 1 Can't!

JEFFREY You can't afford not to. At least for a little while. Just take a little time off. JPD can run itself for a month or so.

You must be torn, but you've got to heal yourself. Got to get you whole. Help me discover Hermaphroditie.

CHRIS 2   Discover Hermaphroditie.

CHRIS 1   Why?

JEFFREY   You're not well.

CHRIS 1   Why do you want me to come with you? We've never been close.

JEFFREY   Maybe in healing you, we'll heal the relationship.

CHRIS 2   Wanted to get to know you, I couldn't find the way.

JEFFREY   You probably don't remember but every now and then you'd read me *The Children's Guide to the Superheroes and Their Gods.*

CHRIS 2   Yes, I do remember.

CHRIS 1   Never enough time.

JEFFREY   I think that's when I decided to be an archaeologist.

CHRIS 2   Jerada.

CHRIS 1   Jerada.

CHRIS 2   Sounds so nice.

JEFFREY   Don't make any decisions about JPD right now, just come with me to Jerada. It's a beautiful little town, there are telephones, you can communicate with New York, if you feel you have to.

CHRIS 1 $300,000, eh. An expensive vacation.

JEFFREY   Who says I won't put you to work. You'll be digging in the earth, sweeping away the sand and washing off bits of pottery.

[*The timer for the quiche goes off.*]

The quiche, finally.

CHRIS 1   I'll say yes to a month and that's it.

CHRIS 2   I'll see how long I stay once I get there.

JEFFREY   Come on, let's get some nourishment.

[*Blackout.*]

• • •

Sada

Bruce Levy

Bruce Levy

Having recently retired his New York–based Bruce Levy Talent Agency, Bruce presently has gone back to his roots in writing and acting, and his film *True Love* is making its way around the festival circuits, including the Woodstock Film Festival and the Miami Short Film Festival, as well as the New York Film & Video International Festival. His new film, *Museum Scandals*, will be shot the early part of 2008. Both films are directed by his partner/wife, Sande Shurin. He currently can be seen in the indie award-winning film *The Definition of Insanity* by Robert Margolis. Bruce started his career in this industry as a set designer and production manager for Drifting Traffic Theatre Company. He also performed in many Off- and Off-Off-Broadway plays and indies at that time. He went on to a recurring role in the TV daytime drama *The Guiding Light*. He switched gears at this point and became the vice president of sales for a Fortune 500–size privately held company. Simultaneously he produced, with Leslie Steinweiss, Betty Neustat's *The Price of Genius* on Broadway, with Sande Shurin directing. He also wrote several additional plays, including *Pool Plays* and *Can You Hear Me Mama*. Combining his business acumen with his experience in all aspects of the performing arts, he opened his own talent agency.

His one-act play *A Moment in Time*, staring Donna Castellano and Roy Arias, became a two-act play, *Sada*, and was presented at a New York theater starring two-time Academy Award nominee Sylvia Miles and star of stage and television Jai Rodriquez. He currently manages, with his wife, the Sande Shurin Acting Studios in New York, which they created together in 1980. They also run a retreat for actors in Woodstock, New York.

···production note···

Sada (pronounced Sayda), in its full form, consists of two acts. In this volume, it is presented as a one-act (act one of the two).

• • •

[*Audience and stage are dark. Sound of a toilet flushing. Sound of water, washing hands. Low lights come up as bathroom door opens and* SADA *shuffles out of the bathroom to the kitchen. She puts a kettle on and takes a frozen bagel from fridge and places in microwave. She goes to phonograph and puts on a 78-rpm record, Al Jolson's "Anniversary Song." She sits at kitchen table and fondles a picture of her deceased husband, Jake, that has been sitting there. She does not hear the sound of a window breaking over the music. A beam of light from a flashlight goes on* SADA's *face as* ANGEL, *a young, sensitively handsome Hispanic boy/man with long hair cups* SADA's *mouth and puts a gun to her head. It is 1:00 a.m.*]

ANGEL   Make a sound and I'll kill you . . . Walk!

[*He pushes* SADA *down the hall towards the living room.*]

SADA   Oy, oy.

ANGEL   C'mon, c'mon! WALK.

SADA   So I'm walking. I'm walking.

ANGEL   Shut up! Not a sound! I'm telling ya! Keep it moving!

   [*Entering living room.*]

   On the floor!

[*He pushes* SADA *to the floor as she groans.*]

SADA   Please!

ANGEL   Shut up! Not a sound. Not a word!

[ANGEL *ties her hands with her bathrobe sash.*]

Let's see what you got here.

SADA [*Groaning.*] Oy, oy.

[*She is having trouble breathing.* ANGEL *ransacking the apartment.*]

ANGEL A lotta shit. Look at this shit!

[*He throws things around.*]

Nothin'!

[SADA *continues to struggle and is having a hard time breathing.*]

You alright there?

SADA I can talk?

ANGEL You alright or not!

SADA I'm an old lady!

ANGEL Alright, shut up!

[*The record comes to an end and the needle can be heard crackling and scratching the record.*]

SADA You shouldn't treat an old . . .

ANGEL SHUT UP! Did I tell you to shut the fuck up!

SADA So here . . . I'm shut!

ANGEL Good.

[*A beat. He continues to ransack.*]

SADA But you should know…

ANGEL JESUS! Are you fuckin' deaf?

SADA Sure a little deaf but…

ANGEL Not a word! NOT A FUCKIN 'NOTHER WORD! Now you hear that?

SADA Oy, now I'm deaf! Not a word. Shut! But maybe you could fix the record. It was our record. Please, before…

ANGEL OK, OK, OK.

[*He fixes the record, then continues to ransack apartment.*]

SADA Thank you.

[SADA *groans and is still having a hard time breathing.*]

But you should know I'm very uncomfortable.

ANGEL Are you stupid? SHUT UP!

[*Silence except for sounds of ransacking and* SADA's *heavy breathing.*]

SADA So…I'm shut again. But still…

ANGEL You want me to gag you?

SADA …you should just know…

ANGEL I can make this worse and gag you!

SADA [*Huffing and puffing.*] OK, so now I'm permanently shut!

ANGEL You're a pisser, mami!

SADA But I still can't breathe.

ANGEL [*Coming over.*] What do you need? Can't have you fuckin' die on me! Ya gonna die on me?

SADA Maybe you can untie?

ANGEL That'll make you breathe?

[*Bell on microwave rings.* ANGEL *jumps and points gun in direction of sound.*]

ANGEL What the fuck!

SADA Nothing, nothing, it's the micro heater...

ANGEL Micro heater? What the fuck is a micro...

SADA ...defrosting an onion bagel.

ANGEL ...wave? Microwave?

SADA You should know I'm an old lady...

ANGEL Not heater...wave. Microwave!

SADA ...and you shouldn't treat an old lady...

ANGEL And you should know that I'm a desperate criminal and you better shut up and stop being stupid.

SADA Oy, oy, please! Who's it gonna hurt? Please.

ANGEL Shit!

[*The kettle whistle goes off. Again,* ANGEL *swiftly points gun at noise.*]

Shit, shit, shit, what's that?

SADA Nothing, nothing, the kettle.

ANGEL What is this, a fuckin' restaurant?

SADA Such a mouth on such a handsome boy! Shame!

ANGEL Alright, alright.

SADA Harmless, a mother... a grandmother I should be... please.

ANGEL Untying her hands. Alright, alright, c'mon, c'mon.

[*She struggles to get up, he helps her.*]

SADA [*Rubbing her wrists.*] Thank you, desperate criminal.

ANGEL A pisser, mami, a real ball-breaker!

SADA You're a good boy.

ANGEL Yeah, good. Sit.

[*Helps her to chair at dining table.*]

SADA I can tell.

ANGEL Now sit. Be quiet... OK? Can you be good? Can you do that?

SADA I'm an old woman. Who am I going to hurt?

[ANGEL *continues to ransack.*]

Oy. Such a mess!

ANGEL [*Finding a jewelry box.*] Garbage!

SADA   [*Agreeing.*] Garbage.

ANGEL   How am I gonna feed my family on this crap?!

[*Throws jewelry.*]

SADA   A nice-looking boy. So this is what you do for a living?

ANGEL   Continuing to look. No... I'm a computer expert, mami. I just do this for fun.

SADA   You made a funny?

ANGEL   Yeah, a funny.

SADA   So you have a family.

ANGEL   Why?

SADA   Why what?

ANGEL   Why do you want to know?

SADA   I already know. You said, "How can I feed my family on..."

ANGEL   Forget it.

SADA   So, I shouldn't know?

ANGEL   Yeah, you shouldn't know.

SADA   Maybe I can help.

ANGEL   Help what? Oh, shit... To shut you up... My old lady, my baby and my sister, Maria. OK? Done? Fuck! You are a pisser, mami!

[ANGEL *continues to ransack apartment.*]

SADA Such language you have!

ANGEL Yeah.

SADA Your baby?

ANGEL My baby.

SADA You're just a baby.

ANGEL If you don't shut the fuck up, I'm gonna show you just what a baby can do. Now shut up! I did you a favor, but I can always tie you back up and gag you, you know!

[*Quiet except for the sounds of drawers opening and things being flung around.*]

SADA So how old?

ANGEL What?

SADA How old?

ANGEL For what?

SADA For what, what?

ANGEL What am I on television here? Is someone gonna jump out and yell, "Hey, asshole, this is *Candid Camera*"? Is this a joke here or something?

SADA Ahhh, Allen Funt!

ANGEL What?

SADA The camera man ... Allen Funt.

ANGEL   Please...I'm losin' my concentration here...give me a break. I got a job to do here!

SADA   Some job...makin' a mess!

ANGEL   It could be worse, you know.

SADA   So how old?

ANGEL   Ahh, shit! Alright. Three now. OK? I hardly know him. They put me away for almost three years for doin' nothin'. So now I gotta make up for lost time. OK? The whole story. Alright? The end!

SADA   Jail?

ANGEL   So now I'll give 'em something! Now I know better.

SADA   So now you know better for the something than for the nothing.

ANGEL   That's right.

SADA   So now you're a big man!

ANGEL   That's right.

SADA   Your father...your mother...can't help you?

[ANGEL *continues to search but perhaps not as frantically.*]

ANGEL   Father? What father?

SADA   Mother?

ANGEL   Maybe she killed herself, maybe not. She was tired of having nothing. Never nothing again.

SADA Your mother would have approved?

ANGEL Maybe not, but at least she would have been taken care of.

SADA Enough, enough, stop the mess! Under the sofa.

ANGEL What?

SADA Stop making such a mess! It's under the pillows in the sofa.

[SADA *surveys the room.*]

The jewelry. Oy...look, look! A shonda.

ANGEL [ANGEL *surveying jewelry.*] Now this is better, mami.

SADA So now you'll go home a hero.

ANGEL Why?

SADA So why not?

ANGEL Why'd you tell me?

SADA I got better in my deposit box. Why not make you a hero? Why not? So now, "desperate criminal," you can stop? Yes?

[*He shakes head and smiles.*]

I can clean up?

[*She walks to kitchen.* ANGEL *follows. He eyes a vase.*]

ANGEL Nice!

SADA Done! Finished!...You said.

ANGEL   Just looking.

SADA   Looking, we don't need. Come . . . [*Waving tea bag.*] A little Lipton from the flow through.

ANGEL   Thanks, mami. You're OK. Nice house you got.

SADA   Thank you.

ANGEL   Sorry I fucked . . . messed it up.

[SADA *puts kettle on.*]

SADA   It died.

ANGEL   Huh?

SADA   The apartment, it died. . . [*Cutting a piece of cake.*] ten years ago, it died. When Jake died it died. Sit, please. Stop looking so good.

  [*Bringing piece of cake . . . tempting him.*]

  Homemade chocolate bobka . . . come . . . sit.

ANGEL   It's nice. It's clean.

SADA   [SADA *walks* ANGEL *to table.*] Yes, clean. I clean. That's what I do. I clean a little, I shop a little, a bistle breakfast, a nice lunch and alone again for dinner. And I clean and watch the TV.

  [SADA *starts towards whistling kettle.*]

  Sit, sit. I feel so stupid watching that thing all the time. A boob. I feel like a boob sitting and watching and waiting.

ANGEL   Waiting for what?

SADA   For what? Mmmmmmm . . . for what? For the carpet to get dirty . . . for the toilet seat to be up . . . for something should happen. [*Serving.*] Milk? Lemon? Sugar? Sit! Please. Sit for an old lady . . . sit.

[*Hesitantly he sits.*]

ANGEL   Maybe just . . .

SADA   I'm Sada Jacobson, how do you do? [*She holds out her hand to shake.*] And you?

ANGEL   Angel.

SADA   She ceremoniously dunks one tea bag for both cups of tea. A little company. What's so bad? A little late all the way around but a little company.

[ANGEL *shovels sugar into his tea.*]

So? . . . Nu? . . . Good?

ANGEL   Very good, mami.

SADA   Too much sugar. Not good for your health. Diabetes, heart disease, hypertension . . . a nice young man like yourself [*Stops herself.*] So you have another profession?

ANGEL   This is what I do.

SADA   You should have another profession.

ANGEL   Yeah.

SADA You make a living this way?

ANGEL Enough.

SADA Your, as you say, old lady?

ANGEL Rosa.

SADA That's a nice name too . . . [*Feeling the words on her tongue.*] Rosa . . . Angel. Jake, my husband . . . gone, my sisters, my brother, most of my friends, all gone. My boy's not good. Heart . . . His heart. A young man and he has a bad heart. Well, maybe not so young by you . . . fifty-nine. You?

ANGEL Me?

SADA How old?

ANGEL Twenty-one.

SADA Twenty-one. So young. Rebecca my daughter-in-law calls once a day, every day. She's good. She tries. It helps. But Ira!

[ANGEL *looks questioningly.*]

My son, Ira, the heart—[*Indicates chest area.*]—never calls.

ANGEL Never calls his mami?

SADA Too busy.

[ANGEL's *questioning look.*]

Accounting. Thirty-five years. He is a very good accountant.

ANGEL He should be good to his mother!

SADA Thank you. This card?

[*Referring to a greeting card on table.*]

ANGEL Valentine's Day, tomorrow.

SADA [*Looking at clock on wall.*] Well, already really, today. It's signed, "With all our love…," but I know the handwriting. It's Rebecca. One son and a pen he can't pick up!

ANGEL That's no way to treat his mami!

SADA Such a nice young man. And you? How long at this?

ANGEL At what?

SADA How long have you been at your line of work?

ANGEL Since about eight or so…

SADA Eight years? That's a long time to climb, break in, make a mess.

ANGEL No, since I'm eight years old.

SADA You been doing… [*She indicates the mess.*] since you were eight years old?

ANGEL Yeah… that's why I'm so good.

SADA Yes, good. A good mess!

ANGEL But no one ever got hurt.

[SADA *gets up and goes for broom from closet.*]

SADA But still… Oy, a life for a little boy!

ANGEL   What are you doin'? Sit...sit...I'll do it.

SADA   And Rosa? She knows?

ANGEL   Sit down.

[*He takes broom away and starts to clean glass.*]

You sit down, mami. Finish your tea.

[*She sits.*]

SADA   She knows?

ANGEL   She thinks I drive a late truck.

SADA   So she doesn't know.

ANGEL   She thinks I went straight.

SADA   Why not?

ANGEL   Tried it.

SADA   And?

ANGEL   Nah, just can't make a decent livin'.

[ANGEL *shyly sweeps.*]

SADA   A long night. Some eggs, a piece of toast? We're all a little hungry.

ANGEL   I just had some bubba.

SADA   Bobka.

[*Starts to prepare food.*]

ANGEL   Bobka...And your husband?

SADA   Jake.

ANGEL   Your husband, Jake. How did he take care of you?

SADA   Ahhh, a good man, Jake. A good provider. Maybe if we had nothing, he'd be doing like you. Who knows. His father was a milliner. Jake was a milliner. But you know what happened to milliners. But OK, we had a little put away. [*Commenting on cooking.*] An egg pancake. A little of this, a little of that...

ANGEL   Bacon? Ham?

[SADA *holds the back of her middle and index finger to her mouth and spits twice.*]

SADA   Sha, sha! But how would you know. You don't know. Kosher. You know kosher?

[ANGEL *shrugs.*]

Jewish. I'm Jewish. No pork, no meat with milk. You...no meat on Friday? Same thing. For what? All these years for what? I wouldn't go to heaven? But still kosher. Kosher I was and kosher I am. But you don't worry. I'll make you nice. Some lox, some eggs, some onions.

ANGEL   Lox?

SADA   You'll like. Wait. You'll like. Oy, such a *punim*. Such a face. A little thin but a mother would be proud.

[*Continues cooking.*]

ANGEL   So what did Jake mill?

SADA   Milliner. You don't know millinery?

[ANGEL *shrugs. She puts a hat on her head, then sits down while onions are cooking.*]

Milliners were people who made hats. Jake was a good milliner. Jake made hats. A respectable trade. Big in his father's day. Good to Jake. But women stopped wearing hats. Jake knew from working with his hands. Pretty things. But you know what happened to anything handmade. And women just stopped wearing hats! We had a little put away but...ah, it was never good after he stopped. He was never good after he stopped. Oy, Jake.

[*Hits chest.*]

ANGEL   My father did shit. Hardly knew him. Think he's dead. My mother did wash, welfare, worked hard...always a broken heart, always in pain. Bastards!

SADA   She did her best?

ANGEL   Yeah, she did her best.

SADA   And that's what counts, she did her best.

ANGEL   She never got to see Angel.

[SADA *gives quizzical look.*]

Angel Jr. The baby.

SADA   Ahhhhh...

[ANGEL *takes out a picture and shows her.*]

Oy, yoy, yoy, yoy, yoy... She would have been so proud. A
little like you. Yes, your eyes, your mouth.

ANGEL   Ya think?

SADA   Yes, of course, look. And this, who is this?

ANGEL   Rosa, my old lady.

SADA   Not so old!

ANGEL   No, my old lady, my...

SADA   I know, I know, a beautiful young girl. A good mother?

ANGEL   Very good. Always readin' 'n' lookin' and findin' out
what's good for Angel.

SADA   A family! A nice family.

ANGEL   Is that Jake?

[*Pointing to a picture.*]

SADA   Ah, oy, my Jake—[*Fondling picture.*]—yes, my Jake...

ANGEL   And this was Ira?

SADA   Jules. My firstborn. A holiday we declared when he was
born. So bright, such a light! Such a tragedy!

ANGEL   What happened?

SADA   Who knows. Today they have names for these things. But
then, one day he was alive the next he was dead. A few
months of heaven we had. A long time ago. This is Jake
and me [*Showing another picture.*] Miss Sada Cohen...before
the Mrs.

ANGEL   Hot!

SADA   What?

ANGEL   You were hot, mami!!

SADA   Ahhh, yes. Miss Sada Cohen soon to be Mrs. Sada Jacobson was real, as you say, "hot." And this one [*Referring to another picture.*] was taken at the beach at Coney Island just before we were married. Jake was handsome and strong. From a good family but he knew his way around. From the Bronx. A little rough around the edges . . . like you. Me? I was a princess from Brooklyn. We met through friends. He was my hero. This day Jake was taking me home from the beach on the subway train. Such a nice day, such fun, we swam, we ate ice cream and hot dogs, we played skeet ball on the boardwalk, you know skeet ball?

[ANGEL *shrugs.*]

You have a ball you throw up a ramp and try to get it into the holes with the most points. Then you take your points and trade them for a prize.

[ANGEL *recognizes game.*]

Well, on this day Jake played and played and played until he was able to get me a big pink stuffed bear. It cost him more than if he would have bought me a bear but he wanted me to have that bear so bad to take home with me. So we get on the subway train and Jake had his arm around me and I was hugging the pink bear when hooligans came onto the train to rob us. They stood at each door of the train and one ruffian went to each person and pushed and shoved and took their jewelry and money. Jake and I were sitting in the corner. Jake drew me closer to him and whispered in my ear. Don't worry, kiss me and make believe we don't notice. Oy, in public we kissed and hugged and I shook and trembled and squeezed the big pink bear tight. The man guarding the door near us had a stump for one of his arms. He was wearing a T-shirt and you could see. At the next stop people tried to run off the train but the men at the doors pushed them back.

[ANGEL *reacts.*]

Yes! And Jake stood up and gently took the man's stump in his hand and said, with such a heavy Brooklyn accent from where I don't know, "Hey, have fun but done hurt nobody too much OK, my friend?" The guy said, "Nahhh, done worry, done tell no one, k"? Jake said, "Who'm I gonna tell"? We got off the train and Jake told the token man and the token man called the police, who boarded the train at the next stop and arrested them. My hero, Jake.

[*Smelling onions.*]

Oy, oy! The onions. [*To stove.*] I always tell Rebecca, don't burn the onions! The egg pancake is never good when you burn the onions. Gentle. It has to be gentle. So . . . I burn the onions! I yell at my daughter-in-law, "It's not good if you burn the onions!" So? Look!

ANGEL   Don't worry, mami. It's fine. Don't worry.

SADA   For what. I have so much to think? I have so much to do?

ANGEL   You doin' just fine, mami . . . He was a good man.

SADA   Jake? Yes, quite a man.

ANGEL   Sounds like you and Jake had it good.

SADA   "Had it good"? We fought, we yelled, we struggled, we had two children, one lived, one died. We had joy, we had pain, we were poor, we were rich and we had love. Yes. Important! We had love . . . trust. Not quite as you say "having it good" but a good life together. We had a good life.

ANGEL   Yeah . . . I want for Rosa and the baby like that. For my sister, Maria.

SADA   Ahhh, you want! I know you want. But to have. To be willing to go through it to have it? That's the big question. The $64,000 dollar one. Because it's never too late.

ANGEL   You think?

SADA   Sada doesn't think, Sada knows.

ANGEL   Nah . . .

SADA   We can cut a little here—[*Indicates his hair.*]—clean you up, teach you a little there, and we'll get you a real job. If you're willing to take the walk, maybe you have Sada to walk with. Easy it may not be, but what is? Jail is?

[*Loud banging at door.*]

POLICE OFFICER BLUM   [*Offstage.*] Open up, it's the police!

[ANGEL *jumps up and takes out his gun.*]

ANGEL   [*To* SADA.] SHHHHHHHH.

POLICE OFFICER BLUM   [*Offstage.*] You there, Mrs. Jacobson? You hear me?

POLICE OFFICER MORELLI   [*Offstage.*] Anyone home?

ANGEL   Shit, shit!!

SADA   [*To* ANGEL.] It's OK. I'll . . .

ANGEL   SHHH, SHHH! It's over . . . oh, man I'm through.

[*Loud pounding.*]

SADA   What are you shushing me?

ANGEL   Ahh, shit! I'm on parole. It's over. Ahh, shit!

POLICE OFFICER MORELLI   [*Offstage.*] Open up or we'll have to break in!

ANGEL   [*To* COPS.] She's all right.

SADA   I'm all right.

POLICE OFFICER BLUM   [*Offstage.*] Who's that?

SADA   This is Mrs. Sada Jacobson.

POLICE OFFICER BLUM   [*Offstage.*] And you, son?

[ANGEL *not sure what to say.*]

SADA   My nephew.

POLICE OFFICER MORELLI   [*Offstage.*] His name! What's your name, boy!

[ANGEL *panics.*]

ANGEL Ummmmm...

SADA Arnold... from Montclair, New Jersey.

POLICE OFFICER BLUM [*Offstage.*] We got reports there was a break-in...

SADA He came all the way from Montclair, New Jersey, and he forgot his key and he couldn't wake me up.

POLICE OFFICER BLUM [*Offstage.*] So he broke your...

SADA So he broke the window and climbed in. He was afraid something happened to me when I didn't answer the door. A good boy!

POLICE OFFICER MORELLI [*Offstage.*] Mrs. Jacobson, let your nephew answer for himself... Your last name, boy?

[*Again,* ANGEL *panics.* SADA *mouths her last name, Jacobson.*]

ANGEL JACOBYSON! [*Like Jacoby and Myers.*]

[*Covering* ANGEL's *mistake,* SADA *opens front door with chain on.*]

SADA I'm all good. Not to worry. See? Ten fingers, ten toes. [*She does a little jig.*]... You see. Fine. All good.

POLICE OFFICER MORELLI [*Offstage.*] OK, Mrs. Jacobson. You take care of yourself.

SADA Yes, of course, thank you. Next time I'll invite you in for a nice piece of home-baked bobka. Good night.

OFFICERS Good night.

[*Footsteps leaving.*]

SADA [*Calling after them.*] Good night. Good night.

ANGEL Shit!!!

SADA A close call!

ANGEL Shit...you don't know. They'd throw away the key this time.

SADA It's over.

ANGEL It's over.

[ANGEL *goes to the door, opens it with chain on and peaks out.*]

I could have been in big trouble!

SADA Mrs. Katz. [*She points to a window across the way.*] She sits at that window. She always knows, she always sees, she always hears. Not that I'm complaining. It's usually good. But she never sleeps. Some privacy one needs every once in an often without her knowing every business every minute. Come, a little egg pancake, a bit of tea, a new outlook...

ANGEL I should go.

[ANGEL *gives her back the stash of jewelry.*]

From my heart, mami.

SADA No, no, please...for an old lady. The toast is cold, the pancake a little micro zap. Give them time to leave. Let them leave.

[*He sits, she heats food in microwave for a few seconds.*]

My Ira's wife, Rebecca, insisted. [*Referring to microwave.*] I wouldn't hear of it. Who needs all this new technology? Women in Europe still wash their clothes on rocks. I lived this long without. Who needs it? But a potato so quick and to heat and defrost such a blessing. Come. Taste.

[ANGEL *tastes.*]

Good?

[ANGEL *smiles but is having trouble eating.* SADA *standing over him.*]

You open, you chew, you swallow... not so bad when you get the knack.

ANGEL   Sorry, mami... I am so sorry!

[*Sitting, he throws arms around her waist and hugs her.*]

SADA   Come... A little music. Jake always was with a little music to lift the spirits.

[*She goes to record player on puts on the* Indian Love Song *and dances around. She changes her hat and looks up.*]

Remember, Jake? Remember this hat? My best dancing hat.

ANGEL   78s... Probably worth a fortune!

SADA   Here. Come here... Come on. You know how to dance?

[*She is swaying and dancing around the room.*]

Sada shouldn't have to dance alone. Come. For Sada.

[ANGEL *shyly gets up and walks towards* SADA. *She takes him in her arms.*]

You know how to dance? ... or like the rolling and the rocking you probably do but like this. Like Jake ... oh, how we danced ... A young girl. A handsome young man. Good music. All is good with the world. Oy, how we danced.

[*She spins a bit.*]

ANGEL   Go get 'em, mami.

[*He gently spins and turns her.*]

You ... Hot! Hot! Hot! Mami ... We gotta get a little more beat ... Ya got something goin' ...

[*There ensues a wonderful spirited, heartfelt dance scene going from the waltz to* ANGEL *doing salsa, double-beating the music, he jumps on the chairs,* SADA *trying to keep up with him, her arms flailing in the air looking more like the Hava Nagila.* SADA *is out of breath.*]

SADA   This is as much beat as Sada can take. You're a good boy. A good boy. Thank you, my son.

[*They sit back down.*]

I know what we need. Come ... A glass of Manischewitz ...

ANGEL   Mana who?

SADA   Manischewitz, Malaga. A wine for the Gods!

[*She pours. They sip, he coughs.*]

ANGEL   God, is this sweet. Nyquil! [*Imitating* SADA.] It's not good for you. Too sweet! Hypertension, diabetes, heart disease.

SADA   [*Laughing.*] A little seltzer spritz will help. A toast.

>   [*They click glasses.*]

>   May the angels watch over my Angel.

>   [*They drain their glasses,* SADA *refills.*]

>   Good, huh?

[*They giggle.*]

ANGEL   Yeah, good cough syrup.

[*Drain glasses again.*]

SADA   Oy, it's hot in here.

[*Fanning self, laughing.*]

ANGEL   [*Filling glasses.*] You think we're hot now. Chug down another.

SADA   So what can you do?

[*Both laughing, both tipsy, both having a good time.*]

ANGEL   What can I do? Ya wanna know what I can do?

SADA   [*Laughing.*] You think that's funny! You can't take care like this all your life.

ANGEL   [*Having a good time.*] Oh yeah? Ya think so?

SADA   So what special talents?

ANGEL   Mmmmm. Now let me think...I'm very good at breaking windows and frightening...

[*Both hysterical laughing.*]

SADA   Yes, very good.

ANGEL   It's a talent!

SADA   Yes, a talent all right. I'll never forget such a talent! But a good heart. A family man. You speak Spanish?

ANGEL   [*In Spanish.*] Yes, of course I speak Spanish, I am Spanish, maybe you couldn't tell.

SADA   You can change words from English to Spanish and visa versa!

ANGEL   This is what I do.

SADA   No . . . this is what you do when you have nothing else. We have to find the something else.

[ANGEL *getting angry.*]

ANGEL   This is what I do. OK? [*In Spanish.*] THE END! FINISHED.

SADA   [*She avoids his anger and gets a book from shelf.*] Here, you read in English, then you tell me in Spanish. You'll see. This is a special talent!

[*She gives* ANGEL *the book.*]

ANGEL   [*Throwing book across the floor.*] I told you this is what I do. I don't read these fuckin' books and I don't do nothing I don't want to do!

SADA   Mmmmmmmmmmm . . . So you choose a book. There are plenty of books. [*Indicates bookshelf.*] You choose.

[*Dead space.*]

Nuuuuuuuuuuuuu.

ANGEL [*Getting up.*] I gotta leave.

SADA You gotta read!

ANGEL [*Walking to door.*] I gotta do nothing! I gotta leave!

SADA But you can't.

ANGEL [*Defensive.*] What do you mean I can't? I'll leave if I wanna leave!

SADA Read. You can't read. You can read? Read. Here read!

ANGEL So? So what? [*At door.*] . . . I'm outta here!

SADA So you leave now, you leave with your pride, but a thief . . . You sit back down!

[ANGEL *releases door knob,* SADA *guides him back in.*]

Sammy Davis Jr. had one eye and learned to sing and dance like a miracle. Sit. Sit. You, with two eyes, can learn to read. Sada will help.

ANGEL I can't, mami.

SADA You went to school?

ANGEL I went to school. Ya think I'm stupid!

SADA Oh no! My Angel is not stupid.

ANGEL I tried. I can't.

SADA   Stupid is the school . . . the teachers to not have you read. For Rosa, the baby, try with me.

[*Nothing.*]

Hello? [*Gently knocks him on the head.*] Is anyone home?

[*Nothing.*]

You know Sada was a teacher.

[*Nothing.*]

A good teacher!

[*Nothing.*]

A very good teacher!

[*Nothing.*]

Knock, knock.

[*Nothing.*]

KNOCK, KNOCK!

[*Gently pushing him.*]

ANGEL   Yeah? Who's there?

SADA   An Angel.

ANGEL   All right . . . an Angel who?

SADA   An Angel who can read and write and take care of his family . . . Yes?

[ANGEL *shrugs*.]

Yes!?

[*They clink and drain wine glasses, tapping the bottoms to get the last drop. A loud amplified voice shatters the silence from the street below. Stark floodlight cuts through the window.*]

BLUM [*Offstage.*] THE PLACE IS SURROUNDED.

SADA Oy, vey...No, no.

ANGEL Fuck, fuck, fuck, fuck.

BLUM [*Offstage.*] Give up, we'll go easy.

ANGEL What a fuckin' idiot I am!

SADA An idiot you are not.

MORELLI [*Offstage.*] Let the hostage go.

ANGEL [*Out window.*] SHUT UP! SHUT UP! SHUT UP!

SADA Nu...I'm a hostage now.

[SADA *opens window.*]

So you're happy now you woke up the whole neighborhood?

ANGEL Fuck!

BLUM [*Offstage.*] Our new information says that Arnold, your so-called nephew, may have a gun. Mrs. Jacobson? What's happening here?

ANGEL I should have went when I could!

[The following scene is a combination of serious confront and humor.]

SADA *[Calling out window across the street.]* So, nu? You happy now, Mrs. Katz?

ANGEL *[To COPS.]* Fuck you! She's fine. Go away.

SADA *[Calling out window across the street.]* You have to put that nose everywhere it doesn't go?

BLUM *[Offstage.]* What's your name, son?

ANGEL *[Out window.]* Go away!

SADA *[To ANGEL.]* Shh, shh. *[To POLICE.]* You see I'm fine. Go. What else?

BLUM *[Offstage.]* We spoke to your son.

SADA *[To COPS out window.]* Ira? You spoke to . . .

BLUM *[Offstage.]* You have no nephew named Arnold from Montclair or anywhere else. Now we need to know what's going on up there.

ANGEL *[To SADA standing at window.]* Fuck, they're not putting me away again. *[To POLICE.]* FUCK, you're not putting me away again! *[To self.]* Fuck this!

SADA Ira? From how do you speak to my Ira?

ANGEL *[To SADA.]* I'm so sorry, mamita.

[He takes out his gun points it at her head, yelling out window.]

All right, ya wanna play rough? I'll play rough!

202 • Bruce Levy

SADA   Don't do that. Are you crazy!! Sit…sit!!! If they saw that! If they see you with that!

MORELLI   [*Offstage.*] Mrs. Jacobson…

SADA   [*Out window.*] Sada, call me Sada.

MORELLI   [*Offstage.*] Why are you trying to protect…

SADA   [*Out window.*] Sada knows you mean well. But today you are making a mistake. If we tell you his real name, will you…

ANGEL   NO! NO!! They'll throw away the key this time.

BLUM   [*Offstage.*] It certainly would help.

SADA   [*Out window.*] My secret admirer has a good reason for not letting you know his name. Give us a few minutes, I'm sure we can work it out.

BLUM   [*Offstage.*] Was that a gun. Mrs. …. Sada?

SADA   A gun? A toy! A friend! A game! Go, please.

BLUM   [*Offstage.*] Sorry, we can't do that, Sada, mam.

ANGEL   OH, MAN!! IT'S OVER. I GOT TO MAKE A RUN FOR IT!

[ANGEL *goes to door and looks out peephole.*]

MORELLI   [*Offstage.*] We need to talk to your admirer there. We'll come up. Let us in this time and then we'll go. You're alright?

SADA [*Out the window.*] Yes! Yes! I should lie? I'm good. I'm fine. The whole neighborhood now knows I'm good and fine. How come you don't? Stop talking, stop waking up the whole neighborhood at [*Looks at clock.*] 2:12 AM.

ANGEL [*To* SADA.] A fuckin' loser. I'm a fuckin' loser.

SADA [*To* ANGEL.] No loser... you are not a loser. [*Out window.*] Officers, what are your names?

BLUM [*Offstage.*] Blum, mam. Officer Blum.

MORELLI [*Offstage.*] Morelli.

ANGEL [*At peephole.*] I'm sure they have the hallway covered.

SADA [*Out window.*] Blum? Blum? A nice Jewish boy doesn't believe Sada?

MORELLI [*Offstage.*] Mam, we're here to protect you. You lied about his name, it looks like he has a gun, for all we know he has a gun to your head. Let us up.

SADA Here... my head...

BLUM [*Offstage.*] Let us in, mam.

ANGEL You don't have a back door or something?

SADA [*To* ANGEL.] Sit! [*Out window.*] Nu? Do you see a gun to my head? Do I sound like a gun to my head?

MORELLI [*Offstage.*] Just let us up, Mrs. Jacobson. We can finish this. Just let us up. We'll talk.

[*The phone rings.*]

SADA [*Out window.*] A circus!! Hold! My phone, it's ringing.

[*Muttering to self, walking to phone.*]

At this time of night, a call. We'll have a party. I can't get a call like a normal person?

[*Answering phone.*]

Hello at 3:00 a.m. in the morning. Who is it?

MORELLI [*Offstage.*] Mrs. Jacobson?

SADA [*Yelling towards window.*] My son, Ira.

ANGEL [*Out window.*] SHE'S ON THE PHONE!

SADA You don't call for two weeks... this is a fine how do you do!

BLUM [*Offstage.*] Mrs. Jacobson, are you all right?

SADA [*Yelling at window.*] Fine, fine... it's my son, Ira.

ANGEL [*Out window.*] Fine, fine... It's her son, Ira.

SADA You know Officer Blum?... How the acquaintance?... Angel... His name is Angel. He's a good boy... Angel's a good boy, Ira.

ANGEL [*To SADA.*] Sorry, mamita, I gotta get outta here.

SADA [*Yelling.*] I'll be right back!... A zoo!

[ANGEL *guides* SADA *towards window.*]

IRA [*Crackling from open phone.*] Mama... where are you? Mama? MAMA!!

ANGEL   One more time, mami...

> [*Puts gun to* SADA*'s head and arm around neck, walking to window, talking to* SADA.]

It's not loaded...

> [*Points gun at ceiling, pulls trigger.*]

But I gotta get outta here.

SADA   [*To* ANGEL.] A good boy. [*Yelling to* IRA *on phone.*] A good boy. You hear, Ira?

ANGEL   [*Out window.*] So here's the gun [*At* SADA*'s head.*] and I gotta get outta here.

SADA   [*Out window.*] It's not loaded, not to worry!

ANGEL   She's not hurt yet.

SADA   I'm not hurt!

IRA   [*Offstage from phone.*] MAMA!!

ANGEL   Just let me go and everybody's happy.

SADA   Everybody's happy.

MORELLI   [*Offstage.*] Yeah, sure with a gun to her head!!

BLUM   [*Offstage.*] Throw down the gun and we'll talk.

ANGEL   This is the talk. This is the deal...

IRA   [*From phone.*] Mama, GET AWAY FROM THE WINDOW. Are you at the window?

ANGEL . . . I walk out. We all forget about it.

SADA [*Out window.*] He's a good boy. Am I all right? I'm as good as good. A toy.

ANGEL [*To* SADA.] I don't think your helpin' here, mami.

SADA [*To* ANGEL.] Let me talk to Ira . . . he should help.

  [*Taking gun, she goes to phone.*]

  Ira . . . I'm here. At the phone.

BLUM [*Offstage.*] Throw down your gun and we'll talk.

SADA [*Removing phone from ear and yelling at window.*] Here, here, the gun.

IRA [*From phone.*] Mama?

SADA [*Yelling back at* IRA.] I have the gun, Ira. A minute. [*Yelling at window.*] Here . . . here . . . so how bad.

[*Showing gun, but she's too far away for the cops to see.*]

IRA [*From phone.*] JESUS CHRIST!! MAMA! IT'S A CORDLESS PHONE! WALK WITH THE PHONE! STOP PUTTING ME DOWN!

MORELLI [*Offstage.*] Throw down the gun.

BLUM [*Offstage.*] We can work this out. No one has to get hurt.

ANGEL [*Out window.*] Oh no. If you get the gun, I go to jail!

SADA [*To* IRA.] Hold.

[*She puts down phone.*]

IRA   [*From phone, screaming at top of lungs.*] MAMA!!!!!

SADA   [*Talks into the air, going to the window.*] OY, A CIRCUS ...

[*Shows the gun to* COPS *out the window.*]

... mit three rings.

IRA   [*From phone.*] MAMA!! PICK UP THE GODDAMN
PHONE!

SADA   [*Yelling towards phone.*] YOU TOO, IRA? LANGUAGE!
[*Out window.*] You see. I have the gun. How bad? [*Yelling at
phone.*] So how bad, Ira? I have the gun!

[*Yelling to everyone.*]

IT'S NOT LOADED!

MORELLI   [*Offstage.*] Then throw it down, Angel.

ANGEL   FUCK!!!!

SADA   [*On phone, complaining.*] Cordless, macro waves, micro
waves, I just get used to one and it's another!

BLUM   [*Offstage.*] C'mon, son.

ANGEL   HOW'D YOU FUCKIN' KNOW MY NAME?

SADA   [*On phone.*] He's good, Ira. All the noise and lights, what
better to do?

MORELLI   [*Offstage.*] We know a lot.

SADA   [*On phone.*] Yes, I'm in the living room. I can't hear you good with all the commotion.

ANGEL   [*Out window.*] Fuck you!

SADA   [*On phone.*] Hold. [*To* ANGEL.] Ira said I'd be able to hear better in the bedroom . . . let's go into the bedroom. [*To* IRA.] Me? Just me? Why just me? He's a good boy. Not to worry. He's not to hurt me . . . Stop screaming!

BLUM   [*Offstage.*] Let's see the gun, Angel. Where is the gun now?

ANGEL   [*Yelling out window.*] Up my ass! Come and get it!

SADA   [*On phone.*] You think in the middle of all this he's gonna take advantage in the bedroom. Ira, is that what you think? . . . What's going on here?

[*Walking to bedroom, swinging the gun.*]

I'm walking . . . I'm walking. Mit the phone, I'm walking. Hold on to your socks! In the bedroom now. I hear you. I'm listening, I'm locking . . . but why? It won't make me feel better [*She locks bedroom door.*] but there. It's locked. But I don't feel any better.

MORELLI   [*Offstage.*] What's goin on up there, folks?

SADA   [*On phone.*] He's a good boy, Ira. [*Yelling through the locked bedroom door to* ANGEL.] Come in, we're talking to Ira. [*To* IRA.] But why can't he come in? [*Yelling through door.*] Angel? You hear me? [*To* IRA.] Hold, I don't think he hears me. [SADA *opens bedroom door.*] Angel . . . come!

IRA [*Over the open phone line.*] MAMA!! CLOSE THE DOOR.
DID YOU OPEN THE DAMN BEDROOM DOOR?
MAMA!! MAMA!!!!!!!! DAMN IT!

MORELLI [*Offstage.*] Everyone healthy? Alive?

ANGEL [*Out window.*] Listen, man. Just turn... turn off all the
lights, stop the yellin'. The lady is safe. Just let me go and
it's over. Really, she's safe. No harm. It's over.

SADA [*Yelling.*] Yes, Ira. I'm safe, in the bedroom. The lights are
on. Yes, the lights are on. Nice and safe... What is wrong
with you, Ira?

BLUM [*Offstage.*] We'll give you safe passage... maybe go light on
a sentence...

SADA Putting phone down and opening the bedroom window.
But he didn't do anything.

ANGEL [*To police.*] But I didn't do anything.

IRA [*Over open phone.*] MAMA? Are you at the window? MAMA,
GET AWAY FROM THE WINDOW. Please, Mama...
Do you hear me!

SADA [*Over phone.*] Stop screaming, Ira! Stop the ruckus... I'm
here. Safe and sound, Ira. He's such a good boy, help. Can
you call them?

MORELLI [*Offstage.*] Where are you, Mrs. Jacobson?

SADA [*Over phone.*] The drapes? The drapes? You're a decorator
now? In the middle of this, a decorator?

MORELLI   Mrs. Jacobson? Sada? Talk. Where are you?

SADA   [*Over phone.*] The drapes are open, they're closed, what makes a difference?

BLUM   [*Offstage.*] If Mrs. Jacobson doesn't press charges . . . and you throw down the gun . . .

MORELLI   [*Offstage.*] Yeah! Throw the friggin' gun out the friggin' window and we can talk. Now! Do it!! Last chance!

SADA   [*Yelling towards open bedroom window.*] Who's pressing charges from my bedroom, I'm speaking.

ANGEL   [*To* COPS.] NO JAIL.

SADA   [*On phone.*] Ira, he's a good boy. Not to hurt him. [*She clicks the gun.*] See, it's not even loaded.

ANGEL   [*To* COPS.] I'll give you the gun. You let me go?

SADA   [*Yelling towards bedroom window.*] He'll give you the gun, let him go! [*To phone.*] Yes, Ira . . . not loaded . . . He's good. He's twenty-one . . . a little break he needs. Not the advantages you had.

ANGEL   [*To* SADA.] Mami, you have the gun? . . . Sada, mam?

SADA   [*Calling to* ANGEL.] Yes, the gun I have [*Pulling the trigger, calling to window.*] I have the gun!

[*To* IRA.]

We danced . . . we danced, we talked, we ate. Just a little break he needs. This is not a bad boy.

BLUM   [*Offstage.*] Angel, hold tight, I'm talking to the sergeant.

SADA   [*Over phone.*] Too late? What's too late? Ira, what's going on? Make a call! What signal? Which signal means what, Ira? You stop them, Ira. Are you crazy? Has everyone gone crazy? Is this a movie? This is not a movie, Ira. YOU STOP THEM, IRA, STOP THEM!!!!

[*She opens door to bedroom, calls to* ANGEL.]

Come in here. ANGEL YOU COME IN!

[SADA *turns lights on and off, not knowing what signal is for what.*]

Lights on, lights off, I don't know what's for what, Ira! You tell me what's for what!

[*The searchlights go out. All is in dark. Glass shattering. Bolts of light as explosions from guns shatter the darkness. The stage is almost in total darkness except for the lights from guns exploding.* SADA's *front door is broken down and light from the public hall slices through the darkness.*]

MORELLI   GET THE SON OF A BITCH!

ANGEL   [*Screaming.*] CAREFUL, YA GONNA HURT HER!!!! DONE HURT HER!

BLUM   MOTHERFUCKER!!

SADA   NO!!! NO!!! ANGEL!!! BE CAREFUL, ANGEL. DON'T HURT MY ANGEL!!

[*"Anniversary Song" starts to play.*]

ANGEL   MAMI, MAMI, CAREFUL, MAMI.

[ANGEL *jumps in front of her and it looks like he takes a bullet protecting her.*]

SADA   NO!! NO!! HE'S A GOOD BOY. CANT YOU SEE!!!!

ANGEL   [*Screaming.*] DON'T HURT MAMI!

[*Music louder.*]

SADA   A GOOD BOY!!!!!!!

[*Gun fire, screams, chaos.*]

[*Fade to black.*]

• • •

5:15
Greyhound

Le Wilhelm

Le Wilhelm

Le Wilhelm's full-length play *Maiden's Progeny: An Afternoon with Mary Cassatt, 1906*, was published by Samuel French in 2006. The publishing house has also published his anthology *Eight Plays from the Heartland*. He has over twenty-five plays published, and his *Missouri Trilogy* is represented by Samuel French as well. He was the recipient of the Florida Council of the Arts grant. Wilhelm, along with producer Kathy Towson, also heads up the award-winning writer's workshop RCL. In addition he has served as guest lecturer for Pen and Brush, guest artist for the Savannah Art's Festival, and has served as a literary judge for a number of writing contests.

5:15 Greyhound was performed at the Harold Clurman Theatre and was a Critic's Choice winner in the Samuel French Off-Off-Broadway Original Short Play Festival.

Directed by Diana LeBlanc:

> **MRS. WHITE**, Jackie Jenkins
>
> **MARY ALICE**, Kristen Walsh
>
> **TOM**, Joseph Arnone

Also directed by Stephen Deighan:

> **MRS. WHITE**, Ann Parker
>
> **MARY ALICE**, Justine King
>
> **TOM**, Andrew Brown

staging notes

The play can best be performed with minimal staging, requiring only a bench where the characters wait for the early morning Greyhound. Although costumes can be from any period, I feel that perhaps late 40s or 50s is best. It is important that the clothing is clean, but it should be apparent the family is poor.

characters

> **MRS. WHITE**, should be in her 40s or early 50s. She is a gentle woman who has led a hard life.
>
> **MARY ALICE**, late teens. There should be a certain innocence about the character.
>
> **TOM**, younger than Mary Alice. A gentle young man, a bit broken.

• • •

[*Sitting on a bench waiting for a bus are three figures. It is night and there is a lantern with them. The figures are* MRS. HOMER WHITE (ALICE), MARY ALICE *and her younger brother,* TOM.]

MRS. WHITE   You packed the scarves I knitted you?

[*Pause.*]

Mary Alice, you packed the scarves, didn't you?

MARY ALICE   Yes, Momma, I packed them.

MRS. WHITE   You sure?

MARY ALICE   You've asked me that at least a half dozen times. You know I did.

MRS. WHITE   I know. I'm just a little jittery, that's all.

MARY ALICE   So am I.

MRS. WHITE   Mary Alice, I just got so much I'd like to say that I can't think of what to say.

MARY ALICE   You'd better get back to the house, Momma.

MRS. WHITE   I know.

MARY ALICE   If he wakes up and finds you not at home, then you'll be in real trouble.

MRS. WHITE   What's he going to do?

MARY ALICE   I don't need to answer that.

MRS. WHITE   It's too late. He can't keep you from getting out of here.

MARY ALICE   If he wakes up and you're not in bed, he'll start looking for you. Then he'll start looking for the rest of us.

MRS. WHITE   You're right.

MARY ALICE   He could find me here before the 5:15 Greyhound arrives.

MRS. WHITE   He sleeps like a log. All night long. He never wakes up in the middle of the night.

MARY ALICE   With bad luck, this'd be the one time he does.

TOM   Even if he did wake up, Mary Alice, he'd never think we were here.

MARY ALICE   Proves what you know. There ain't that many places we'd be.

MRS. WHITE   Actually, I left a note on the table saying that Aunt Louise had taken a turn for the worse. I figured I'd tear it up when I got back home.

MARY ALICE   Why didn't you tell me before?

MRS. WHITE   I didn't want you to know that I'd written a lie.

MARY ALICE   Oh, Momma.

MRS. WHITE   You know how I feel about lying.

MARY ALICE   It's important that he never know you helped me get away.

MRS. WHITE   I just don't care anymore, Mary Alice.

MARY ALICE   You'd change your mind once he started in.

MRS. WHITE   It's not that bad. He's not. It's just that you got to get out of here. And if you don't leave soon, you never will.

MARY ALICE   I could always leave.

MRS. WHITE   But you won't. You're young still. You still got the heart to leave. You still have the spirit. Few more years his preaching will have you so beaten, you'll never make it free.

MARY ALICE   That's silly talk, Momma.

MRS. WHITE   I know from whence I speak.

MARY ALICE   Momma.

MRS. WHITE   I'm leaving now. You know I love you, Mary Alice.

MARY ALICE   I know, Momma.

MRS. WHITE   And I'll miss you something awful.

MARY ALICE   I'll miss you, too.

MRS. WHITE   You'll write.

MARY ALICE   You know I will.

MRS. WHITE   And you'll let me know if you need something.

MARY ALICE   I will.

MRS. WHITE   Your aunt Hester and uncle Frank have promised they'll take care of you till you can get on your feet.

MARY ALICE   I know.

MRS. WHITE   You got their address, right?

MARY ALICE   Right here. I got everything.

MRS. WHITE   Oh my.

> [*She sobs and hugs her daughter.*]

I love you.

MARY ALICE   I love you.

MRS. WHITE   [*Quickly exiting.*] God be with you. Tom, you get home as soon as the bus comes.

[*She exits. There is a long silence.*]

MARY ALICE   Bless her heart. I hope she forgives me.

TOM   What are you talking about?

MARY ALICE   Shh. Wait until she's out of earshot.

TOM   What are you doing, Mary Alice?

MARY ALICE   Be quiet!

TOM   What's going on?

MARY ALICE   Tom, you listen to me. Here's the address in Kansas City of Aunt Hester and Uncle Frank.

TOM   What are you giving it to me for?

MARY ALICE   'Cause you're going.

TOM   What?

MARY ALICE   You got to get out of here.

TOM   Momma wants you to go.

MARY ALICE   I know. And I will. Someday I will. But not this time. You're catching this bus.

TOM   This don't make no sense.

MARY ALICE   Don't argue with me. You're 18 years old, and Pa keeps you cooped up like a 10-year-old. You ain't allowed to do nothing. You ain't never even had a girlfriend.

TOM   I don't want one.

MARY ALICE   How would you know? He pulled you out of school in the fourth grade.

TOM   I'll get out of here. I'll come to you.

MARY ALICE   No. You're going. I know how it is around here. Now, my suitcase is all packed with your stuff, even the scarves are dark ones that you can use, and I snuck into your room and got your things, and I've saved a little money from sewing and you'll find a new pair of shoes. And new store-bought underwear.

TOM   I can't go!

MARY ALICE   Tom, don't start saying you can't. You're going.

TOM   Why do I have to go first?

MARY ALICE   Because I said so.

TOM   You're afraid to go, aren't you?

MARY ALICE   So what if I am? I'm a girl. I'm allowed to be afraid.

TOM   I'm afraid, too.

MARY ALICE   Oh, baby, of course you are. But you got to do it, Tommy. You got to do it for me.

TOM   Why?

MARY ALICE   Because I love you.

TOM   Momma's going to be mad if you don't leave and I do.

MARY ALICE   And Papa's going to be mad either way. But you're going.

TOM   Mary Alice, if I do, and after I find myself some work and a place to live, if I send for you, will you come?

MARY ALICE   I'll do my best to come, Tommy.

TOM   That's not good enough.

MARY ALICE   If you send for me, I'll come.

TOM   You promise.

MARY ALICE   Yes.

TOM   In the name of Jesus.

MARY ALICE   In the name of Jesus, I give my word.

TOM   What's it going to be like out there?

MARY ALICE   I don't know.

TOM   Will it be better?

MARY ALICE   I think so.

> [*Moment.*]

> Yes, it'll be better. It's got to be better.

> [*Moment.*]

> Here's the money Momma gave me for the ticket.

TOM   Geez, how much does the ticket to Kansas City cost?

MARY ALICE $9.85.

TOM   Mary Alice, there's over $120.00 here.

MARY ALICE   She's been saving up. She wanted to make sure I'd be okay. Now I want you to take it so you'll not need anything at first.

TOM   Mary Alice, there's enough here for both of us to get a ticket. And still have money left. We can both go.

MARY ALICE   I can't do that.

TOM   Why not?

MARY ALICE   I just can't. Momma'd be all alone.

TOM   Either you come with me or I'm not going.

MARY ALICE   Tom.

TOM   I think you're afraid to come. I think that's it.

MARY ALICE   Both of us can't go. We can't both leave Mother.

TOM   Yes, we can. I think she'd be happy.

MARY ALICE   Tom, I packed all your clothes.

TOM   Aunt Hester'll give you some of her old things until we get on our feet.

MARY ALICE   This won't work.

TOM   You don't know unless you try.

MARY ALICE   I just can't.

TOM   Then I can't either. Let's get on back home.

MARY ALICE   Tom, don't do this.

TOM   We need each other. I can't do it without you and you can't do it without me. But together, we might be able to make it.

MARY ALICE   You ain't going to go if I don't go?

TOM   *No*, I'm not.

MARY ALICE   I'm worried about Momma, Tommy. But if it's the only way to get you out of here, I guess I'll have to go.

TOM   Maybe Momma'll be better off not having to worry about us.

[*He hears the bus.*]

Listen, I hear the Greyhound coming. We got to wave the lantern so it knows to stop.

MARY ALICE   Tommy, I'm so afraid.

TOM So am I.

MARY ALICE I can see the lights.

TOM Way down the road.

MARY ALICE Isn't it amazing how far you can see the lights in the night.

[*The lights go out as they wave the lantern for the oncoming bus, and then the lantern itself goes out. Blackout.*]

• • •